THE THEOLOGY OF HOLINESS.

DOUGAN CLARK, M. D.

Professor of Systematic Theology and Church History in
Earlham College, Richmond, Indiana.

1ˢᵗ WORLD
LIBRARY
Literary Society

The Theology of Holiness

Dougan Clark

© 1st World Library – Literary Society, 2004
PO Box 2211
Fairfield, IA 52556
www.1stworldlibrary.org
First Edition

LCCN: 2004091178

Softcover ISBN: 1-59540-624-7
eBook ISBN: 1-59540-724-3

Purchase *"The Theology of Holiness"*
as a traditional bound book at:
www.1stWorldLibrary.org/purchase.asp?ISBN=1-59540-624-7

1st World Library Literary Society is a nonprofit
organization dedicated to promoting literacy by:

- Creating a free internet library accessible from any
computer worldwide.
- Hosting writing competitions and offering book
publishing scholarships.

Readers interested in supporting literacy
through sponsorship, donations or
membership please contact:
literacy@1stworldlibrary.org
Check us out at: www.1stworldlibrary.org

The Theology of Holiness

contributed by the Charles Family
in support of
1st World Library Literary Society

TO THE MEMORY OF
MY FATHER AND MOTHER,
DOUGAN AND ASENATH CLARK,
BOTH FOR MANY YEARS APPROVED
MINISTERS IN THE FRIENDS' CHURCH,
AND BOTH LONG SINCE DEPARTED
TO BE WITH CHRIST, THIS
BOOK IS LOVINGLY
Dedicated.

CONTENTS

CHAPTER I.

ENTIRE SANCTIFICATION A NECESSITY.

Science is a systematic presentation of truth. Theology is the most important of all sciences. It is the science that treats of God and of man in his relation to God. It is a systematic presentation of revealed truth. As the basis of Astronomy is the universe of worlds revealed by the telescope, and as the basis of Geology is the crust of the earth, so the basis of Theology is the Divine revelation found in the Holy Scriptures. The Theology of Entire Sanctification, therefore, is a systematic presentation of the doctrine of entire sanctification as derived from the written word of God. Such a presentation we hope - with the help of the Holy Spirit, which we here and now earnestly invoke - to attempt to give in this book. May God bless the endeavor, and overrule our human weakness, to the glory of His Name. Amen.

It is a lamentable fact that there is a large class of Christians to whom the subject of entire sanctification is a matter of indifference. They hope, with or without sufficient reason, that their sins are forgiven. They propose to live moral and useful lives, and trust, again with or without sufficient reason, that they will go to heaven when they die. The subject of holiness does not interest them. They suppose themselves to be doing well enough without it.

There are others claiming to be Christians, to whom the subject is even positively distasteful. It is an offence to them. They do not want to hear it preached. They regard those who claim it as cranks. They look upon holiness meetings as being hotbeds of delusion and spiritual pride. They turn away from the whole subject not only with indifference, but with disdain.

There are still others, and these God's children, as we may charitably believe, who do not even regard holiness as a desirable thing. They assert that it is needful and salutary to retain some sin in the heart as long as we live, in order to keep us humble. It is true that they are never able to tell how much sin it takes to have this beneficial effect, but a certain amount they are bent on having.

Another class takes the opposite view. They regard holiness as very desirable, and a very lovely thing to gaze upon and think upon, but they also regard it as quite impossible of attainment. They hope to grow towards it all the days of their lives, and to get it at the moment of death. Not sooner than the dying hour, do they believe any human being can be made holy. Not till death is separating the soul from the body can even God Himself separate sin from the soul. The whole doctrine of entire sanctification, therefore, they regard as a beautiful theory, but wholly impossible as an experience, and wholly impracticable as a life.

In general terms, we may say that carnal Christians, as described by Paul in I. Corinthians 3:1-4, are opposed to the doctrine of entire sanctification. "The carnal mind is enmity against God," and the carnal mind is irreconcilably opposed to holiness. This opposition may take one of the forms already described, or, possibly, some other forms which have been overlooked, but the root of the hostility is the same in all. Wherever "our old man" has his home in a Christian's heart, there entire sanctification will be rejected.

But we must not forget that there are many exceptions. There are thousands of sincere, believing hearts in all Christian denominations, in whom inbred sin still exists, but not with the consent of the will. They are tired - very tired of the tyrant that rules them, or of the ceaseless struggles by which, with God's added and assisting grace, they are enabled to keep him under. They long for deliverance. They are hungering for full salvation, and rejoice to hear the message of entire sanctification through the baptism with the Holy Ghost and fire. The Lord bless all these hungering multitudes, and give them the desire of their hearts by saving them to the uttermost, and may their numbers be vastly increased, so that the banner of Christ's church may everywhere be unfurled - the banner on which is inscribed the glorious motto of Holiness to the Lord.

Now we meet all objections to the doctrine of entire sanctification - whether in the form of indifference, or dislike, or undesirableness, or impossibility - with the simple proposition, It is necessary. If this proposition can be established, all objections, of whatever character, must fall to the ground, and the eager cry of every Christian heart must be, How can I obtain that priceless blessing which is essential to my eternal bliss, which is indispensable, and without which I shall never see the Lord?

For this is the language of the Holy Ghost in Heb. 12:14, "Follow peace with all men, and holiness without which no man shall see the Lord," and in the Revised Version, "Follow after peace with all men, and the sanctification without which no man shall see the Lord." This can mean nothing short of entire sanctification, or the removal of inbred sin. And, surely, it is hardly necessary to argue the question as to the indispensableness of this blessed experience, in order to gain an entrance into heaven. Everyone will admit that God Himself is a perfectly and absolutely holy Being, and He has ever told His followers in all ages, "Be ye holy for I am holy" - making His own perfect and entire holiness the sufficient reason for requiring the same quality in His people. And, although the holiness of the highest created being will always fall infinitely short of that of the Infinite God, as regards quantity, it will be the same *in quality*, for Jesus tells us, "Be ye perfect even as your Father in heaven is perfect," not, of course, with the unmeasurable amount of perfection which appertains to Him, but with the same kind of perfection so far as it goes. And again in Rev. 21:27, we are told that "There shall in no wise enter into it" (the heavenly city) "anything that defileth, neither whatsoever worketh abomination or maketh a lie." Heaven is a holy place, and occupied with none but holy inhabitants.

But if holiness of heart is a necessity in order that we may reach the blissful abode of the glory land, when is this stupendous blessing to be obtained? It is by no means, thoughtlessly, that I write obtained and not attained. It is very generally spoken of as an attainment, and this form of expression has a tendency to discourage the seeker by magnifying the difficulty of receiving this blessing. The thought contained in the word attainment is that of something earnestly striven for, struggled after, persistently pursued with much labor and toil and effort, until, at last, the coveted prize is attained. A very few of the multitudes who went to California, soon after gold was discovered there, attained fortune; but it was after years of hard labor and privation and hardship. The majority died on the way, or while mining for the precious metal, or returned as poor as they went.

On the other hand, the idea of an obtainment is simply that of a gift. And entire sanctification is precisely a gift, "merely this and nothing more." It is not received by struggle, nor effort, nor merit of our own; it is not a great and laborious enterprise to be undertaken; not the fruit of a long journey or a perilous voyage; not by doing, nor trying, nor suffering, nor resolving, nor achieving, but by stretching out the hand of faith and taking. Praise the Lord.

And, therefore, we ask again when is this indispensable gift to be obtained? The Roman Catholic and the Restorationist answer, in purgatorial fire, or in some kind of a second probation after death. But the Holy Scriptures tell us absolutely nothing either of a purgatory or a post-mortem probation. On the contrary, they clearly teach us that our destiny for all eternity is to be determined in one probation, which is allotted to us in the present life. Let no one suppose, for a moment, that he can be made fit for heaven at any time, nor in any place, nor by any means, after he has left this mundane sphere. "Behold, now is the accepted time; behold, now is the day of salvation."

But all the Calvinistic churches by their creeds, and also a large portion of the membership of Arminian denominations, without regard to their creeds, if asked when are we to obtain entire sanctification as an essential meetness for heaven, would answer, at death. The prevailing idea on this subject, among Christian believers, seems to be as follows: First, through repentance toward God and faith toward our Lord Jesus Christ, we are converted. Our past sins are pardoned, and we are born again. After that, our sole business is to grow in grace, and by this growth to approach nearer and nearer to the standard of entire sanctification, but never even suppose that we can reach that standard until the moment of death.

Now, grace is the gift of God, and we cannot, possibly, grow in grace until we receive it. And we can never grow into grace, but grow in it after we get it. We can grow, it is true, in the grace of justification to a limited degree and for a limited time. The degree is limited because of the presence of inbred sin, which is the great, if indeed, not the only hindrance of growth. The time is limited in most cases, at least, because if the justified Christian is brought to see the need and the possibility of entire sanctification, and yet fails, as so many do, to enter into the blessing, because of unbelief, he is very prone either to backslide, in which case, of course, there will be a cessation of growth, or, like the Galatians, he will submit to the bondage of legalism, and after having begun in the Spirit, he will seek to be perfected in the flesh; in which case Paul's verdict to that beloved church was not ye are growing in grace, but, "ye are fallen from grace."

It is plain, therefore, that we can never grow into the blessing of entire sanctification. That blessing is to be received by faith, as the gift of God in Christ Jesus and through the Holy Spirit; and when the grace has once been obtained in this manner, then we can grow in it indefinitely and for a lifetime, possibly even for an eternity. Growth in grace is a most blessed thing in its right place, and when rightly understood and experienced, but it can never bring us to the death of the old man, nor to the experience of entire sanctification.

And as growth cannot do this, neither can death. Death is nowhere mentioned in Scripture as a sanctifier. Death can separate the soul from the body, but to separate sin from the soul is a work which God can only do. Jesus Christ is our sanctification, and the Holy Spirit is our sanctifier, and even if the work is performed in the article of death, it is still the Holy Spirit and not death that performs it. And if He can perform it in the hour and article of death, where is the hindrance to His performing it a week, a month, a year, or forty years before death - if only the conditions are fulfilled on our part. Do we say that He cannot perform it before death; then where is His omnipotence? Do we say that He will not do it before death; then where is His own holiness? In either case, we dishonor God and rob ourselves of an inestimable and indispensable blessing. God save us from such folly.

Scripture, reason and experience, therefore, all unite in the sentiment that entire sanctification is to be sought and obtained now, and if now, then it is to be obtained instantaneously, and if instantaneously and now, it follows, also, that it is to be obtained by faith, and from these premises the further conclusion is logically deducible, that we cannot make ourselves any better in order to receive it, but that we must take it as we are. And so we arrive at and adopt the pithy precept of John Wesley, "Expect it by faith - expect it as you are -

expect it now."

In these remarks we have necessarily anticipated some things which belong more accurately to the next chapter; but we are not seeking so much for a perfectly methodical arrangement, as for a clear and Scriptural presentation of the subject. And we proceed to affirm now that entire sanctification is not only essential as the condition of entering heaven, but that it is also necessary for the highest results of the Christian life on earth. It is not only an indispensable blessing to die by, but, if we would fulfill our Father's will in this world, it is indispensable to live by.

But before leaving entirely the subject of growth in grace, having demonstrated, as we trust, that we can never grow into entire sanctification, we ought, perhaps, to explain what we mean by the statement that we can grow indefinitely in that precious grace after, and not before, we receive it. Entire sanctification has two sides or aspects. It has a positive side and a negative side. Its negative side is the removal of inbred sin, and is, therefore, a matter of subtraction. And herein, we may remark in passing, is a characteristic difference between entire sanctification and regeneration. The latter is a matter of addition, because it implies the impartation of a new life to the soul which has hitherto been "dead in trespasses and sins." Now in this negative aspect of entire sanctification there can be no growth. If a heart is pure it cannot be more pure. If it is free from sin it cannot be more free from sin. An empty vessel, as some one has said, cannot be more empty. There can be no increase in purity.

But the positive side of entire sanctification is perfect

love, and this is a relative expression. It does not mean that all who possess it must have an equal amount of love. Perfect love to each individual is just his own heart - not some one else's heart - being filled with love. One individual may have a greater capacity of loving than another, just as he may have a greater capacity of seeing or of working. Perfect love in a child would not be perfect love in a man; and perfect love in a man would not be perfect love in an angel. And perfect love may increase in the same individual so that what is perfect love today may not be perfect love to-morrow. As we commune with God and work with Him, as we get more and more acquainted with Christ and With the Holy Spirit, and see more of the infinite attractions of the Triune God, how is it possible that we should not love Him more and more? "There will never be a time in earth nor in Heaven," says the late Dr. Upham, "when there may not be an increase of holy love." On the positive side of entire sanctification, then, there may be and will be growth indefinitely and everlastingly. And this is the true growth in grace, about which much more could be said, but we leave it for the present, to resume our main theme of the necessity of entire sanctification in this life as well as the life to come.

We make a definite statement as follows, viz: No Christian can do all that God would have him do, nor enjoy all that God would have him enjoy in this world, without the grace of entire sanctification. In the beautiful language of metaphor the Saviour says, "I am the true Vine and My Father is the husbandman. Every branch in Me that beareth not fruit He taketh away, and every branch in Me that beareth fruit He purgeth it that it may bring forth more fruit." And again, "Herein is My Father glorified that ye bear much fruit: so shall ye be My disciples." Now the abundant fruit requires for its production the abundant life, and these are both found in the Lord Jesus Christ. "I am come," says He, "that ye might have life (in regeneration) and that ye might have it more abundantly" (in entire sanctification). The abundant life and the abundant fruit, therefore, can only be found in connection with purity of heart.

It is doubtless *true* that every living branch, that is to say, every justified and regenerated believer, may and should and must, if he would retain his religion, bring forth some fruit. And it is precisely these branches that are bearing fruit, whom the Great Husbandman "purges" - sanctifies - that they may bring forth the more abundant fruit by which He Himself shall be glorified. And here we might rest our case with a Q. E. D., but another remark or two will be in place.

The late Lord Tennyson could perceive, with the genius of a poet, the intimate connection between purity and power. He puts into the mouth of Sir Galahad, one of his heroes, these beautiful words, viz:

"My strength is as the strength of ten,
Because my heart is pure."

Now one of the most common complaints among Christians of all denominations, is because of their weakness and their leanness. And yet nothing is clearer than that God has promised to make His people strong, that He has commanded them to be strong in the Lord, and that not to be strong is even blameworthy, not to say criminal in His sight. The reason, then, of our weakness and our leanness and the meagreness of our fruitage, can be nothing else than because we do not fulfill the conditions on which He promises to make us strong. One of these conditions, and an indispensable one, is that we be entirely sanctified. It is they that know their God, both in conversion and entire sanctification, both in pardon and purity, that shall "be strong and do exploits." Beloved, if you would accomplish the work that God has given you to do, and not have to regret its non-accomplishment in eternity, even if you are saved so as by fire, seek and find that which is the essential condition, and ask at once to be wholly sanctified.

And if you would have the fullness of joy, even the joy of an uttermost salvation, the peace that passeth understanding, the fellowship with the Father and with His son, Jesus Christ, the sealing and anointing of the Spirit, the white stone and the new name, the abiding presence of the indwelling Comforter, then pray that the very God of Peace may here and now sanctify you wholly. Amen.

CHAPTER II.

ENTIRE SANCTIFICATION OBTAINABLE.

This would seem to follow as a necessary corollary from what has been said in the preceding chapter. If entire sanctification has been proved to be not a matter of option but a matter of necessity; if we cannot attain to the highest results in Christian privilege, nor in Christian enjoyment, nor in Christian service without this blessed experience, and if, at the end, we cannot be admitted into the celestial city unless we possess it, surely we cannot doubt for a moment that our gracious Heavenly Father has provided a way by which this indispensable requisite both for time and for eternity may be received.

But before discussing this proposition in detail let us have a clear understanding of what is meant by entire sanctification, and, as a preliminary, let us study a few simple theological definitions.

In the first place, my reader will have no difficulty in believing that I fully accept the Arminian doctrine of the universality of the atonement. The sacrifice of Christ is sufficient for the salvation of all mankind, and its benefits are offered to all. "He tasted death for every man." But it does not follow that all men will be saved, and this for the reason that the atonement is not unconditional but conditional. It is offered to all, and all are invited and entreated to accept it. But it is available only in the case of those who believe. "He that believeth shall be saved, and he that believeth not shall be condemned." A universal atonement, therefore, does not by any means imply a universal salvation.

Redemption is a term of broad and varied application. It is either general or special. In one sense it is as broad as atonement. Atonement is for sin; redemption is from sin and from all the sad results of sin. In its more special meaning it is applicable only to those who accept the atonement. For these it implies release from the bondage of the will under the law of sin and death, or justification and regeneration. It brings also release from the power and existence of depravity or entire sanctification. It promises, in the future, the complete glorification of the saints in body, soul and spirit at God's right hand, and the deliverance of the creation itself from the "bondage of corruption into the liberty of the glory of the children of God."

The first condition on which the benefits of the atonement are offered to the sinner is repentance. Both the Saviour Himself and His forerunner began their public ministry with words of like import, viz: "Repent ye and believe the gospel." Repentance does not mean penance - not a voluntary sacrifice in our own will for an expiation of sin - nor is it merely sorrow for our past sins, although "godly sorrow" is one of the elements of true repentance. The sorrow of the world may produce remorse, that continual biting which tortures the soul of the lost; but remorse is not repentance, and the sorrow of the world worketh not life but death. True repentance involves a change of mind, a change of purpose, a change of will, and implies not only a godly sorrow for sin - sorrow not only because the sin has resulted in physical or mental or financial or reputational disaster - but because it has grieved the Spirit of our God; and it implies not only sorrow for our sin but the determination to forsake it as well. It is the afterthought, and involves both regret for what we have done and the purpose to do so no more.

The next, and specially indispensable, condition for receiving the benefits of the atonement is faith. This means nothing more nor less than taking God at His word. We are assured that without faith it is impossible to please God, for he that cometh to God must believe "that He is, and that He is a rewarder of them that diligently seek Him." "Faith is the substance of things hoped for," because it makes them real. It is "the evidence of things not seen" because it convinces the mind of their actual existence. It is true that all men believe something, and, therefore, that all men have faith. It is not true that all men believe God, and, therefore, not true that all men have saving faith.

And here we must make a distinction. Faith is often said to be the gift of God, and in the sense of the grace of faith, or the power of believing, this is true. But the act of faith is the actual exercise of the power of believing, which God has given us. It involves the putting forth of the choosing power of the human will, that we may accept the salvation which is offered us. God has given to us all the faith faculty, just as He has given to us the seeing faculty. In the one case, as in the other, we are responsible for the exercise of the faculty thus given. The proper object of the seeing faculty is the world around us, with all its multiplicity of existences. We may open our eyes and see or we may close them and fail to see. The proper object of the faith faculty is truth, and especially gospel truth, the truth of salvation through a crucified and risen Lord. We may exercise our believing power and accept this great salvation or we may close our faith-eyes, and fail to see and believe, and this to our eternal loss.

For God commands us to believe and holds us responsible for obedience to that as to all other of His commands. The fact of the command involves the power to obey. Our will, therefore, our choosing power, must be put on the believing side, and not on the side of unbelief. It is not that we are required to believe without evidence. It is that our depraved hearts are not willing to believe when the evidence is ample. And, therefore, our eternal destiny is made to hinge on our obedience to the positive command, "Believe on the Lord Jesus Christ." The great and crying sin of our fallen humanity is unbelief. It is this that has sundered us, as a race, from our union with God, and it is faith which is to be the bond by which we may again be reunited to Him. "He that believeth not the Son is condemned already."

Repentance and faith are the conditions on which God promises to give us the grace of justification. This is pardon for all our past sins. God, for Christ's sake, looks upon us as though we had not sinned. He accounts us just, for Jesus' sake, although we are not just in reality. And herein it is that gospel justification differs from legal justification. The individual who is accused of crime and who is brought into court and determined, by a jury of his peers, not to be guilty, is at once acquitted and released from all penalty. He is justified solely on the ground of his innocence. But no man ever has been or ever will be justified in the court of heaven on the ground of his innocence. Every responsible human being has broken the law of God. "All have sinned and come short of the glory of God." And none of those who have broken the law can be justified by the law, that is to say, not one. The law justifies those, and those only, who keep it. None of us have kept it, not one of the race of men save only the man Christ Jesus. The law condemns all those who break it. All the race of men have broken it save only the man Christ Jesus. Therefore, all are under condemnation. But condemnation is incompatible with justification. Therefore, again, "by the deeds of the law shall no flesh be justified."

Are we not, then, in an absolutely hopeless condition? We should be so but for Christ. But, blessed be God, "He hath found a ransom." "All we like sheep have gone astray; we have turned every one to his own way, and the Lord hath laid on Him the iniquity of us all." Jesus Christ "Himself bore our sins in His own body on the tree." And so it comes to pass that we can be freely justified by His grace, not because of our innocency but because He bore the penalty in our stead. He took the place which was rightfully ours and that is on the cross. He procured for us the place which was and is rightfully His, and that is at God's right hand. He suffered what we deserved, and by that very suffering He made us partakers of what He deserves. Glory forever to His Holy Name!

By the redemption that is in Christ Jesus, therefore, justice is satisfied, and the penalty of the broken law is removed. God is infinitely merciful, but He is also infinitely just. He loves the sinner with a boundless love, but He hates the sin with a boundless hate. He is of purer eyes than to behold iniquity, and will not look upon sin with the smallest degree of allowance. His mercy and His love may compassionate the sinner, but this will be of no avail so long as His justice is against him. "Shall not the Judge of all the earth do right?"

But in the marvelous plan of salvation by a crucified and risen Lord, both the attributes of mercy and justice are enlisted on behalf of the sinner. The mercy of God pardons Him, the justice of God justifies Him, and all for Jesus' sake. "Mercy and truth have met together, righteousness and peace have kissed each other." "God can be just and the justifier of him that believeth in Jesus." "If we confess our sins He is faithful and just to forgive us our sins." And in accordance with the way of salvation which He Himself has devised, we can now plead with Him that He would be unjust not to forgive us when we have complied with these conditions. And so we arrive at the conclusion that justification is an act of God's grace by which our sins are pardoned for the sake of Jesus Christ. And this act is instantaneous. God does not pardon sins gradually, nor one at a time, nor by piecemeal, but to every one who repents and believes, He utters the gracious language, "Thy sins, which are many, are all forgiven thee." As if by a single stroke of the recording angel's pen, the whole dark record is blotted out forever. "As far as the east is from the west so far hath He removed our transgressions from us." Glory.

Regeneration is a work of grace which always accompanies justification. God does not justify a sinner without, at the same time, giving him a new life. This new life is a spiritual life imparted to the soul, which before was dead in trespasses and sins, by the Divine energy of the Holy Ghost. If a sinner should be pardoned, without, at the same time, receiving a new nature, he would inevitably fall into sin again. His lifetime on earth would be spent in sinning and repenting. But our merciful Father having for Christ's sake looked upon him as just and righteous, when he was not so in reality, now bestows upon him a new nature which is just and righteous. He makes him a partaker, indeed, of the Divine nature, and that is a nature which is holy and just and good. And this is the new birth. Men may be full of physical life and of intellectual life, but until they are born from above they are totally destitute of spiritual life. Regeneration, therefore, is that act of God's grace by which we are born again.

Adoption is the reception of the newly justified and regenerated believer into the family of God. No longer enemies, nor even strangers and foreigners, those who have accepted Christ as their Saviour, now receive the adoption of sons. They become the children of God by faith in Jesus Christ. This is their pedigree and they rejoice to declare it. A human governor or ruler may pardon a guilty criminal, and grant him a reprieve, but he never takes him into his own family. He may forgive the guilty one, but he cannot bestow upon him a new nature, nor can he consent to recognize him as a brother or a son. But God not only remits the sins of those whom He saves, He not only delivers them from wrath and from punishment, but He gives them a new nature by which they can respond to His love, and He takes them into His own household as children and heirs, yea, as joint heirs with Jesus Christ. "Ye are all the children of God by faith in Jesus Christ."

The witness of the Spirit is something not easily defined, but it is well known by those who experience it. It is an impression or consciousness wrought into the mind of the believer by the Holy Ghost, which gives him the satisfactory assurance that he is a child of God. Before this, he believes, now he knows. This witness, therefore, expels doubt and infuses into the heart of the new-born child of God, a calm, definite and indisputable persuasion that all is now right between himself and his Heavenly Father. "The Spirit Himself beareth witness with our spirit that we are the children of God." "Ye have received the Spirit of adoption, whereby we cry, Abba, Father." "And because ye are sons, God hath sent forth the Spirit of His Son into your hearts, crying, Abba, Father."

Now the graces that have been mentioned, namely, justification, regeneration, adoption and the witness of the Spirit, are all received co-instantaneously. They always accompany each other, and whoever has one of them has them all. The witness of the Spirit, it is true, is not always a constant experience. It may be intermittent, but, nevertheless, whenever it is present, it accompanies or attends the other experiences to which we have alluded. And we may add that all these graces are but different aspects of the same salvation and are properly and conveniently designated, in common language, by the single term conversion, which term, therefore, must be understood to include and imply justification, regeneration, adoption and the witness of the Spirit. It is proper, also, in this connection to remark that conversion is always a definite and instantaneous event, and never a prolonged process. Just so certainly as every human being that comes into this world has a definite, natural birthday, so every one that comes into the kingdom of God has a definite, spiritual birthday. Some people do not know when their natural birthday occurs, nevertheless, they know that they have been born. Some Christians do not know when their spiritual birthday occurs. Nevertheless, they know that they have been born again. Conversion is the crossing of a definite line out of Satan's kingdom into God's kingdom. There is no half-way ground, there is no neutral territory, there is no place where a man can truthfully say, I am neither converted nor unconverted. One moment he is out of the ark of safety, the next moment he is in it.

Entire sanctification is an act of God's grace by which inbred sin is removed and the heart made holy. Inbred sin or inherited depravity is the inward cause of which our outward sins are the effects. It is the bitter root of which actual sins are the bitter fruits. It is the natural evil tendency of the human heart in our fallen condition. It is the being of sin which lies back of the doing of sin. It is that within us which says No, to God, and Yes, to Satan. It exists in every human being that comes into the world as a bias or proclivity to evil. It is called in the New Testament, the flesh, the body of sin, our old man, sin that dwelleth in me, and the simple term sin in the singular number. In the Old Testament it is called sin and iniquity. "Behold," says David, "I was shapen in iniquity and in sin did my mother conceive me." And when the Seraph brought the live coal and laid it upon the mouth of Isaiah, the prophet, his words were, "Lo, this hath touched thy lips and thine iniquity is taken away and thy sin purged."

Now all Christian denominations are agreed as to the real existence of this inbred sin and also as to the fact that it is not removed at conversion. "This infection of nature doth remain," says the Anglican Confession, "yea, even in them that have been regenerated." Most church creeds, indeed, give no reason to expect, and most Christian believers do not expect to be rid of sin till near or in the hour of death. And it is regarded as serious heresy in some quarters for a man to either preach or claim that the blood of Jesus Christ does really cleanse from all sin.

But God has in every age and in every dispensation required His children to be holy. And to be holy signifies the destruction or removal of inbred sin, nothing more and nothing less and nothing else than that. How this is accomplished will be discussed further on, but here we say that the removal of innate depravity is entire sanctification, and that God has most surely made provision in the atonement of Jesus Christ for the removal of innate depravity. Therefore, He has made provision for entire sanctification, and, therefore again, this wondrous grace is obtainable. Inbred sin goes back to the fall of man in the garden of Eden. If not as old as the human race, it is at least as old as the fall. Since sin entered through the beguiling of our mother, Eve, by the serpent, inbred sin has existed as a unit of evil in every child of Adam and Eve. The only exception is the man, Christ Jesus, the God man, the Divine man, the promised seed that should bruise the serpent's head. But as He, the Lord Jesus Christ, was manifested to destroy the works of the devil, and as inbred sin is one of the works of the devil, therefore its destruction is provided for in the atonement, and, therefore, still again, entire sanctification is obtainable.

The simplest meaning of the word sanctify is to separate or to devote to sacred uses. It has this signification nearly always in the Old Testament and in a few passages in the New. In other words, whatever is consecrated is sanctified in this limited sense. But from the primary meaning is easily derived its secondary and prominent meaning, of separation from all sin, inward as well as outward, and this is what Paul calls being sanctified wholly. It is entire sanctification as distinguished from partial sanctification. This latter appertains to all Christians, and is technically so used in the New Testament. The former is the experience of those, and those only, from whom inbred sin has been removed.

Dougan Clark

CHAPTER III.

ENTIRE SANCTIFICATION IN PATRIARCHAL TIMES.

For the first twenty-five centuries after the creation of man, he was without a written law. So far, at least, as the descendants of Seth are concerned, the government, during those early times, seems to have been patriarchal. The father of a family retained his authority over his children and his children's children so long as he lived, and when he died, the branch families did not separate, but continued their allegiance to some other patriarch, usually the eldest son of the former. A number of families under their respective patriarchs constituted a tribe, and from the family patriarchs was selected a prince for the whole tribe. Among the antediluvian patriarchs were Adam, Seth, Enoch and Noah. Those after the flood were Noah, Abraham, Isaac, Jacob and each of the twelve sons of Jacob. After Jacob's death, it is most likely that Joseph acted, in some sense, as the prince of the tribe during his lifetime. Then came slavery and oppression and deliverance through Moses, and the giving of the law.

As God's revelation to man has been progressive, first just a few faint streaks of light that usher in the dawn, then broad daylight and sunrise, and finally the meridian splendor of the noontide, we are not to expect, in these early times, the full and distinct teaching on the subject of holiness, which we find in the Mosaic law, in the writings of the prophets, and especially and super-eminently in the New Testament. The word holy does not occur in the book of Genesis, and the word sanctify is found only once, where Jehovah blessed the seventh day and sanctified it.

And yet there are, even in these patriarchal times, several narratives of extreme interest, which give us glimpses, at least, of the purpose of God that His people should be holy, and we even find intimations of His method of sanctification, by conferring it as a second experience upon His already saved children, as is so clearly revealed in the New Testament.

"And Enoch walked with God; and he was not, for God took him." Such is the record in Genesis, but when we turn to the eleventh of Hebrews, the faith chapter, we find that "by faith Enoch was translated that he should not see death; and was not found because God had translated him, for; before his translation, he had this testimony that he pleased God." Now, if Enoch, even amid the wickedness of antediluvian ages, walked with God and pleased God, and was translated that he should not see death, there surely can be no reasonable doubt that he was a holy man, an entirely sanctified man, and hence one whose sins had been washed away in the blood of the lamb, that was "slain from the foundation of the world."

"Noah was a just man and perfect in his generations; and Noah walked with God." The prophet Amos exclaims most pertinently, "Can two walk together unless they be agreed?" It is certain, therefore, that God and Noah were agreed, but God, who is infinitely pure and holy, can never be agreed with any person or anything that is unholy. Hence, whatever may be the proper signification of the word perfect, as applied to God's children in Old Testament times, we can scarcely avoid the conclusion that Noah was a holy man, an entirely sanctified man, and this notwithstanding his subsequent error in regard to drinking too much wine, of whose ill effects we may, charitably, suppose he may have been, up to the time of this sad experience, ignorant.

Abraham dwelt with his father, Terah, who was an idolater, in Ur of the Chaldees, when he received the call of God to go entirely away from his kindred and his father's house, and depart into a land of separation, a land which the Lord would show him. He obeyed the call, and this typifies conversion. He went out not knowing whither he went, but only knowing that the Lord was leading him. At his first move, he was accompanied by his father. And he came out of his native land, it is true, but not yet into the promised land. "He came to Haran and dwelt there," or to give the record in full, "And Terah took Abraham, his son, and Lot, the son of Haran, his son's son, and Sarai, his daughter-in-law, his son Abram's wife, and they went forth with them from Ur of the Chaldees, to go into the land of Canaan; and they came unto Haran and dwelt there."

Continuing the account in his dying oration, the martyr Stephen says, "And from thence when his father was dead, he removed him into this land, wherein ye now dwell," but in Genesis the statement is, "And Abram took Sarai, his wife, and Lot, his brother's son, and all their substance that they had gathered, and the souls that they had gotten in Haran, and they went forth to go into the land of Canaan, and into the land of Canaan they came." The last tie of nature was sundered when the old man died, and then Abram took the second step, which brought him into the promised land. There are two distinct stages in his experience before he reached the place, which God designed him to occupy. And these we may as well regard as typical, if nothing more, of the first experience under the gospel - that of regeneration - and of the second experience as well, which is entire sanctification.

In the history of Abraham, a very beautiful and mysterious episode occurs, and that is the story of his transient but highly important meeting with Melchizedek, after his successful expedition against the kings, who had despoiled Sodom and carried away his nephew, Lot. The sacred narrative is as follows, viz.: "And Melchizedek, king of Salem, brought forth bread and wine, and he was the priest of the Most High God. And he blessed him and said, Blessed be Abram of the Most High God, possessor of heaven and earth; and blessed be the Most High God, which hath delivered thine enemies into thine hand. And he gave him tithes of all." No other mention is made of Melchizedek until David writes the 110th Psalm, and this was nearly one thousand years after Abraham. The Psalmist writing by inspiration, and alluding beyond all reasonable doubt to the Messiah, says, "The Lord hath sworn and will not repent, Thou art a priest forever after the order of Melchizedek." And then, again, the inspired record drops Melchizedek out of sight, as it were, for another thousand years, and then once more brings him to the front in the Epistle to the Hebrews, where he is described in glowing language as "first being by interpretation King of righteousness, and after that, also, King of Salem, which is king of peace; without father, without mother, without genealogy (R. V.) having neither beginning of days nor end of life, but made like unto the son of God, abideth a priest continually."

Comparing, then, the different allusions to this most remarkable personage, the following inferences seem fairly deducible therefrom: (1) Melchizedek, being made like unto the Son of God, is preeminently the Old Testament type of the Lord Jesus Christ in his kingly and priestly offices. Both Melchizedek and Christ are priests, and yet the former is not of the chosen family. He is a Canaanite. He is, unquestionably, greater than Abraham. Of his origin, his ancestry and his descendants, we have no account. He brought forth bread and wine. So did his antitype at the Last Supper. The priesthood of Melchizedek was before that of Aaron. Aaron was a Levite, and Levi paid tithes to Melchizedek in Abraham, his ancestor. And the author of the Epistle to the Hebrews argues most conclusively that since Melchizedek was without beginning or end, and greater than Abraham, and with a priesthood that existed centuries before the Levitical priesthood was instituted, therefore Christ, his great antitype, who is from everlasting to everlasting, and who hath an unchangeable priesthood, is to abolish the Aaronic priesthood, whose institution was for a temporary purpose, and was fulfilled when Christ came, who was a priest not after the order of Aaron because He belonged to another tribe, but a priest forever after the order of Melchizedek.

But Melchizedek was not only a priest, he was also a king. And it was not only in his everlasting priesthood, but in his regal office also, that he was a type of the Messiah. David was a prophet and a king, Ezekiel was a prophet and a priest, Jesus, only, combined in His own person the three offices of prophet, priest and king.

Now, if Melchizedek was priest of the Most High God, if he was greater than Abraham, if he was a type of Jesus Christ in His kingly and priestly offices, it is impossible not to regard him as a holy man. He was cleansed from all sin. He was sanctified wholly. He was made like unto the Son of God, and the Son of God is eternally holy. Praise His name. It is, surely, cause of devout thankfulness, that even in those primitive and patriarchal times, when the earth was full of wickedness and violence, that even then God had His witnesses to experimental and practical holiness.

Before leaving this point of the eternal priesthood of Christ, let me remark that it was a sad day for His Church when the idea became prevalent, that ministers of the gospel are in any official sense to be regarded as priests. This serious error may have been derived, in part, from Judaism and, in part, from paganism. It has become incorporated in the creed of the Roman Catholic Church, and the Greek Church as well, and has been productive of the most disastrous results. Among the deliverances of the Council of Trent, held at intervals from 1545 to 1564, and the last Council, which Romish authorities regard as of binding authority, are the following sentences, quoted by the late A. A. Hodge, in his Outlines of Theology: "Whereas, therefore, in the New Testament, the Catholic Church has received, from the institution of Christ, the holy, visible sacrifice of the Eucharist; it must needs, also, be confessed that there is, in that church, a new, visible and external priesthood, into which the old has been translated. And the sacred

Scriptures show, and the traditions of the Catholic Church have always taught, that this priesthood was instituted by the same Lord, our Saviour, and that to the apostles, and their successors in the priesthood, was the power delivered of consecrating, offering and administering his body and blood, as, also, of forgiving and retaining sins."

It is to be feared that not all Protestants are entirely clear of this same idea of the priesthood of the ministry, and that, in thought, at least, many substitute this for the true priesthood, which appertains to all believers. Now, the office of a priest is to stand between God and man. He mediates, and this Jesus did both by propitiation and continues to do, forever, by intercession. "He ever liveth to make intercession for us." He "offered one sacrifice for sins forever." If He has an unchangeable priesthood, and has already offered Himself as a sacrifice, sufficient for the sins of all mankind, the benefits of which each and every one may obtain on the simple condition of repentance and faith, what possible need can there be of any human priesthood to come between God and the sinner? Says George Fox, "Friends, let nothing come between your souls and God, but Christ," and we say Amen.

To sum up on this particular point, we may say that the ancient priesthood, both of Melchizedek, the Gentile, and of Aaron, the Jew, with his descendants, were nothing more than types; and a type can have no real existence after the antitype has come. Therefore, there is no place for a human priesthood under the Christian dispensation. We are taught in Holy Scripture that no one can come to God except through Christ, but we are also taught that all are invited, and all may come directly to Him. All the officers belonging to the New

Testament Church, whether ministers, deacons, presbyters, bishops, elders, or even apostles, are described not as priests but "messengers, watchmen, heralds of salvation, teachers, rulers, overseers and shepherds." Their function is to preach the word, to teach, to rule, but never to mediate. It is clear, therefore, that ministers as such are not priests.

But we must not forget that, in a very important sense, all Christians are priests. But this is through Christ and in Christ, the one great and eternal High Priest. They are priests because they are in Christ. And not only priests, but kings as well. And not only kings and priests, but prophets as well. All these blessed privileges are theirs, solely by virtue of their union and fellowship with Christ, who, in a mystical and spiritual sense, makes them to be partakers of His own priesthood, His own royalty, and His own prophetic office.

Thus we hear Peter exclaiming, under the inspiration of the Spirit, "But ye are a chosen generation, a royal priesthood, a holy nation, a peculiar people."

And again: "Ye also, as lively stones, are built up, a spiritual house, an holy priesthood, to offer up spiritual sacrifices acceptable to God by Jesus Christ." Precisely. If we are priests, we must perform the functions of a priest, and one of these functions is the offering of sacrifice. What, then, are the sacrifices which are to be offered by the Christian Priest? Certainly, not any expiatory or meritorious sacrifices. These are, forever, precluded by the fact that Christ hath offered one sacrifice for sins forever. Nothing can be added to, and nothing can be subtracted from, that infinite and all-sufficient offering.

The first sacrifice to be made by the Christian priest is the surrender of his own body, with all its appetites, organs and capabilities, to God. Listen to Paul.

"I beseech you, therefore, brethren, by the mercies of God, that ye present your bodies a living sacrifice, holy, acceptable unto God, which is your reasonable service." Your bodies, because if you are Christians, you have already presented your hearts; your bodies, because through the body, too often temptation enters into the soul and leads it to actual sin. Your bodies, because of their wonderful mechanism and their equally wonderful activities. If surrendered to the Lord, He makes them the very thing they were originally designed to be, namely, the obedient servants of the soul, and the soul is already His own obedient servant, so that when the soul commands and the body obeys, both are working for God, and when the soul says Go, and the body runs hither and thither, both are going upon God's errands.

It will be observed that the body is to be presented a living sacrifice, not a dead one. All its boundless activities are to be given up to God. The expression, no doubt, implies that the whole man, described by the apostle, with his inspired trichotomy, as spirit, soul and body are to be consecrated unto God, to be His, and His forever, and henceforth to be ready to be, to do, and to suffer all His blessed will.

The command is yield yourselves, not a certain portion of your time, nor a certain portion of your money, nor a certain portion of your effort, nor your sins, nor your depraved appetites, nor your forbidden indulgences. You cannot consecrate your alcohol, nor your tobacco, nor your opium, nor your card-playing, nor your dancing, nor your theatre-going to God. He wants none of these things. All actual and known sins must be abandoned at conversion. Consecration is for a subsequent and a deeper work. None but a Christian believer can thus present his body unto the Lord. Sinners may repent, but Christians are enjoined to "yield themselves unto God, as those who are alive from the dead;" not as those who are "dead in trespasses and sins." Whatever surrender the sinner may and must make in order to be saved, the believer must make a deeper, fuller, more complete surrender, of a different character and for a different purpose. That purpose is that he may be wholly sanctified, filled with the Spirit, and used to the utmost extent of his capacity for the glory of God. Consecration means yielding yourselves unto God. When you yield yourself you yield everything else. All the details are included in the one surrender of yourself.

And remember, also, that your consecration is not to God's service, not to His work, not to a life of obedience and sacrifice, not to the church, not to the Christian Endeavor, not to the Epworth League, not to any organization, not to the cause of God; it is to God Himself. "Yield yourselves unto God." It is, therefore, a personal transaction between a personal human being and a personal God. Your work, your obedience, your sacrifice, your right place and your allotted duty, will all follow in due time. The next sacrifice to be made by the Christian priest, is that of testimony and thanksgiving. "By Him, therefore," says the author of the Hebrews, "let us offer the sacrifice of praise to God continually, that is, the fruit of our lips, giving thanks to His Name."

And the next priestly offering of the Christian is a holy

life, for the inspired author goes on in the next verse, "But to do good, and to communicate forget not; for with such sacrifices God is well pleased." Offer, then, beloved, the body, with the soul and spirit; offer the fruit of the lips and offer the fruit of the life, and you will walk worthily of your priesthood. Glory!

The patriarch Jacob had two distinct and well-defined experiences about twenty years apart. The first of these was at Bethel, when, in loneliness and anguish of mind, he was plodding on his way toward Mesopotamia to escape the vengeance of his brother Esau. This vengeance was not causeless, and Jacob lay down upon the ground with a stone for a pillow, not only distressed in mind from fear and anxiety, but also, we may well suppose, not altogether free from the condemnation of a guilty conscience. But Jacob was a man who had faith in God's promises, even if he did not always obey His commands. And when he lay down to sleep under the open sky, in a state of mind, sad, forlorn, fearful and contrite, God was watching over him, and when he awoke from the wondrous vision there vouchsafed to him, he perceived that God was in the place, and he found that he himself, also, was a new man. Now he could not only believe intellectually what God had said, but he could and did enter into covenant with Him, taking Jehovah for his God, and vowing the tenth or his income to be given to Him. This was such a change of mind and heart as constituted a real conversion.

When, after the many mercies and many trials that fell to his portion whilst dwelling with his uncle Laban, and after the lapse of two score years, he was returning to his father's house, no longer poor and lonely, but with flocks and herds and wives and children, again he was encountered by the fear of his brother Esau who was approaching him with four hundred men. Then it was that there "wrestled a man with him until the breaking of the day." Note it was the man wrestling with Jacob - and the man was the angel, - Jehovah, the pre-existent Christ - and the object of his wrestling was to get the Jacob nature, the old man, the body of sin, out of Jacob. But Jacob resisted, until by a touch the Divine wrestler made it impossible for him to resist any longer. Now he had to cease his wrestling but he could still cling, and he could still cry, "I will not let thee go until thou bless me." Jacob's will was now firmly set upon the blessing; he could ho longer resist the will of the Blesser, but one thing more he had to do, and that was to tell his name. I am Jacob - supplanter, sinner, and then He blessed him there; Jabbok means extinguishment, and Jacob's self-life was extinguished there. He told his name, and in the telling lost it. No longer the supplanter - but Israel, the prince, the prevailer, the overcomer, and Israel was now a wholly sanctified man. Beloved, tell God your name - sinner - seek with fixed determination for the blessing of holiness, fulfill the conditions, and you also shall prevail, and your name will be changed from sinner to saint, priest, prophet, king, having the blessing of entire sanctification, and the Blesser Himself in the person of the Indwelling Comforter. Praise the Lord!

CHAPTER IV.

ENTIRE SANCTIFICATION IN TYPE.

The Mosaic dispensation was legal, ceremonial and typical. "The law having a shadow of the good things to come," says the author of the Hebrews. But a shadow always points to a substance; and so far as holiness is commanded, and so far as it is shadowed forth in the ceremonial law, we shall find that there is a corresponding substance and reality in the gospel of Christ.

In the first place, if we study carefully the provisions of the Mosaic law, we shall be struck with the many forms of ceremonial uncleanness described therein, and with the "divers washings," not only of the "hands oft," but of the whole body, and of "cups and pots, brazen vessels and of tables." All these point to the fact that God will have a clean people, and a clean people is a holy people. The same thing is vividly exhibited in the distinction between clean and unclean animals, the one kind to be used as food, and the other to be disused. Of land animals, only such as both chew the end and divide the hoof, might then be eaten. And of aquatic, only such as have both fins and scales were to be accounted clean. There can be no doubt that this restriction in regard to food is full of meaning. God help us all as Christian believers to distinguish between the clean and the unclean in a spiritual sense, and not to forget that God will have His people now pure in heart, clean in soul, holy both within and without.

The seal of the covenant with Abraham was circumcision, and this became the perpetual rite by which his descendants were admitted to the rights and privileges of that covenant. "Every male child shall be circumcised." But this rite was an outward symbol of "a circumcision not made with hands, in the putting off of the body of the flesh, in the circumcision of Christ" (Col. 2: II. R.V.) And in Romans 2: 28-29, we are told that "He is not a Jew, which is one outwardly; neither is that circumcision which is outward in the flesh; but he is a Jew which is one inwardly; and circumcision is that of the heart, in the spirit, and not in the letter; whose praise is not of men but of God." Beloved reader, may you and I know what it is to experience the inward circumcision, made without hands, even the putting off of the body of the flesh. And this is entire sanctification. In the consecration of Aaron and his sons to the priests' office, not only were they to be adorned with holy garments for glory and for beauty, not only was the breast-plate to be set with twelve kinds of precious stones, but the plate for the mitre was to be made of pure gold, and engraved with the motto "Holiness to the Lord." This was to be always upon the forehead of the High Priest, and must signify that Aaron was to be the holy priest of a Holy God, and that the law required a continuous holiness, as most assuredly the gospel does also.

Now, in the most important sense both the priesthood and the sacrifices were typical of Christ. In the mediatorial work of redemption, he was both the priest and the victim. He offered Himself. And no one will deny that He was holy, harmless, undefiled and separate from sinners. The holy priest, under the law typified the holy priest, who is a priest forever after the order of Melchizedek. But under the gospel dispensation all Christians are priests. "But ye are a chosen generation, a royal priesthood, a holy nation, a peculiar people." And we are priests, not for the purpose of expiation, for expiation was completed by the Lord Jesus Christ, when He "bore our sins in His own body on the tree," but priests to offer up "spiritual sacrifices acceptable to God through Jesus Christ." And every such priest must needs be continuously holy.

The "spiritual sacrifices" which the Christian priest must offer are, as previously stated, (1) his body, with all its members and capacities. The heart was given to Christ at conversion. It is, however, largely through the body that the soul is led into sin, and it is through the body, also, that the soul must perform its work for Christ, so long as soul and body are united in probation. Hence, the Apostle exclaims in the twelfth of Romans, "I beseech you, therefore, brethren, by the mercies of God that ye present your bodies a living sacrifice, holy, acceptable unto God, which is your reasonable service." The Christian must offer (2) also his continual testimony. He must "hold fast the confession of his faith without wavering." "By him, therefore, let us offer the sacrifices of praise to God continually, that is, the fruit of our lips giving thanks to His name." And, finally (3), the Christian priest must offer the sacrifice of a holy life. "But to do good, and to communicate forget not, for with such sacrifices God is well pleased." Beloved, let us ask ourselves if we are constantly offering as a holy priesthood, a consecrated body, a confessing tongue and a godly life. Amen.

This subject has already been alluded to under a different head, but it will bear repetition.

In the ceremonial used under the law for the cleansing of the leper, we find an impressive type or symbol of holiness. Leprosy is most clearly and strikingly a type of inbred sin. It is loathsome, unclean, incurable, fatal and hereditary. The leper was driven from society; he could not dwell in the camp nor in the city. He was an outcast. None must be permitted to approach him. They must be warned off by the despairing cry "unclean, unclean." Nothing can be conceived more desolate or more hopeless than the condition of the leper, unless it be, indeed, the sinner who is an "alien from the commonwealth of Israel, a stranger to the covenants of promise, having no hope and without God in the world."

But to the leper, in many instances, came the glad "day of cleansing." He might not come into the camp, until the priest went forth to him. The priest and no one else could pronounce him clean. And none but Christ has any authority to tell the sinner that he is converted, or the believer that he is sanctified. A clean bird must be slain over living water, another bird dipped into this water flies away toward heaven with bloody wing; the leper is sprinkled seven times, to denote the completeness or perfection of his cleansing, with blood by means of hyssop and scarlet wool bound to a stick of cedar; he must wash his clothes; he must pass a razor over his whole body, and bathe the whole body likewise in water. Certainly, all this needs no explanation. Surely, here is atonement by blood, and cleansing by the washing of water through the word, as plainly described as symbolic language can utter it.

All the bloody sacrifices of the Jewish law, the daily sacrifice both morning and evening, the paschal lamb, the Day of Atonement, the offerings at the various feasts, and innumerable sacrifices offered for individuals or for the whole people, the guilt offering, the sin offering, one for what we have done, the other for what we are, the peace offering, the burnt offering, these, also, all point to the Lamb that was slain from the foundation of the world. In all the sacrifices which we have named, a life was taken and blood was shed. "Almost all things are, by the law, purged with blood, and without shedding of blood is no remission."

But turn now to the New Testament, and read that "It is not possible for the blood of bulls and goats to take away sins." Read again, "If the blood of bulls and goats, and the ashes of an heifer sprinkling the unclean sanctifieth to the purifying of the flesh, how much more shall the blood of Christ, who through the eternal Spirit offered Himself without spot to God, purge your conscience from dead works to serve the living God." Read again, "In Him we have redemption through His blood" - "Having made peace through the blood of His cross" - "Ye who are far off are made nigh by the blood of Christ" - "Being now justified by His blood" - "That He might sanctify the people with His own blood" - and especially "The blood of Jesus Christ, His Son, cleanseth us from all sin."

Here, I insert a quotation from that saintly man, Dr. Edgar M. Levy. "When an oblation for sin was offered up under the old dispensation, the priest was commanded to dip his finger in blood, and to sprinkle it seven times before the Lord. This denoted the perfection of the offering. Nor would the blessed antitype come short of the type. Seven times, at least, did our Lord pour forth His precious blood. He was circumcised and there, of necessity, was blood. He was buffeted on the mouth, and by such brutal hands, that this must needs have been attended with blood. He was scourged, and from Roman scouring there was, of course, blood. The crown of thorns was driven into His precious temples and, surely, this was not without blood. The sharp nails penetrated into His hands and feet, and again there was blood. And one of the soldiers, with a spear, pierced His side, and forthwith came thereout blood and water."

The blood of Jesus, then, is the procuring cause of our sanctification as it is of our justification. Glory be to His Name forever for the precious, cleansing blood. And every Christian can heartily join in the immortal hymn of Toplady on the "Rock of Ages," and especially with the rendering now frequently given to the conclusion of the first stanza, viz.:

"Let the water and the blood
From Thy wounded side which flowed,
Be of sin the double cure
Save from wrath - and make me pure."

The pure olive oil is mentioned many times in Scripture, and was used for a great variety of purposes. In typology, however, it has special reference to the office work of the Holy Spirit. He is distinctively the Sanctifier, and to be filled with the Spirit is designated by the Apostle John as "the unction" or "the anointing." The holy anointing oil was to be sprinkled upon the tabernacle and all its sacred vessels. It was also poured upon the heads of prophets, priests and kings, as a necessary qualification for the discharge of their respective offices. There can be no doubt but that this use of the anointing oil and the sweet perfume, which none were permitted to imitate or counterfeit, has a direct typical reference to holiness. The sacred writer, indeed, says as much. "That they may be most holy; whatsoever toucheth them shall be holy." And as all Christians are kings and priests unto God, it is necessary that they also be anointed with the Holy Spirit, as their types in the Old Testament dispensation were anointed with the outward oil. "Be ye clean that bear the vessels of the Lord." A priest must be holy.

We have already spoken of leprosy as a type of inbred sin, and of the requirement of blood-shedding in the cleansing of the leper. But before that cleansing was complete, the anointing oil, also, was to be applied to the leper, who was healed of his malady. As the priest had already touched his ear, his thumb and his toe with the blood of the sacrifice, so now he touched the same parts also with the oil. First, the blood; afterwards, the oil. And thus it is in the wondrous plan of salvation through the Lord Jesus Christ. First, atonement for guilt and to secure pardon; afterwards, the Holy Ghost baptism for complete cleansing. First, justification through the blood; then entire sanctification through the Spirit.

The anointing oil was also to be applied to the ear, the thumb and the toe of Aaron and his sons in their consecration to the priesthood and, finally, poured upon their mitred heads that it might reach the beard and the skirts of the garments, but by no means touch the flesh. And so, beloved, we must be touched with blood and oil as to our spiritual ears, that we may take heed how we hear and what we hear; and as to our hands that they may do the work of God in all righteousness, and goodness and truth; and as to our feet, that they may run swiftly and beautifully upon the errands of redeeming love; and, at last, upon our heads and running down overall the person to purify and energize the whole man, that we may be "ever, only, all for Him." Praise the Lord. And this can never happen while the flesh, the carnal mind, is still alive.

Jesus Christ Himself, the Son of God and the Son of Man, He who was holy, harmless, undefiled and separate from sinners, was, nevertheless, anointed with the Holy Ghost as a needful qualification for His mediatorial work.

In the synagogue at Nazareth, He read part of the sixty-first chapter of Isaiah. "The Spirit of the Lord God is upon me: because the Lord hath anointed Me to preach good tidings unto the meek; He had sent Me to bind up the broken-hearted, to proclaim liberty to the captives, and the opening of the prison to them that are bound; to proclaim the acceptable year of the Lord" - and here He ceased His quotation abruptly, without saying a word about "the day of vengeance of our God." It was now a day of grace, not a day of vengeance. But to those who will not accept this grace, that terrible day of vengeance will surely come. Jesus was anointed, and He was holy. His anointed followers must also be holy. They must seek and find the baptism with the Holy Ghost and fire, they must be sanctified wholly. To be baptized, and filled and anointed with the Holy Ghost is the privilege and duty of all God's children. If we would belong to the royal priesthood, we must be cleansed from the defilement of sin.

Dougan Clark

Finally, we will allude to the fire symbol. Gold is spoken of in Scripture as tried in the fire. So of silver. "He" (Christ) "shall sit as a refiner and purifier of silver." The precious metals will endure the fire, but "dross and tin," as well as reprobate silver, will and must be consumed. The baptism with the Holy Ghost and with fire is a sin-consuming baptism. Fire is a great purifier. It makes the substance which is subjected to it pure through and through, and not like anything cleansed by water, pure as to its surface only. "Our God is a consuming fire." Oh, beloved, let us give up to the fire all that is for the fire. Let all depravity, all inbred sin, all tendency to depart from God and yield to Satan, be burned up in this fiery baptism. May God put upon all His pardoned children not the blood-mark only, but the fire-mark also.

CHAPTER V.

ENTIRE SANCTIFICATION IN PROPHECY.

The Major Prophets are Isaiah, Jeremiah, Ezekiel and Daniel. The twelve prophetic books in the Old Testament following the book of Daniel are called the Minor Prophets. In the writings of both classes we find many allusions and predictions as to the entire sanctification of believers in the gospel dispensation and under the reign of Messiah or Christ.

The sixth chapter of Isaiah is usually regarded as his call to the prophetic office. Whether this be so or not, it records a very wonderful experience of that grand man, and a remarkable type of the baptism with the Holy Ghost as described in the book of Acts.

It is quite evident that Isaiah was a converted man before he wrote his first chapter. In that he laments the sins of the Israelites and the Jews, all of them God's chosen people, though now divided into the two kingdoms and these often at variance, shows the utter futility of their own efforts to regain the favor of God, by observances and sacrifices and ceremonies, and then tells them how to be converted as plainly as any gospel minister in our own day would be able to do. He shows them that the way of salvation is by repentance and faith, and by trusting to the unmerited mercy of God. Hear him: "Wash you, make you clean; put away the evil of your doings from before mine eyes; cease to do evil; learn to do well; seek judgment; relieve the oppressed; judge the fatherless; plead for the widow. Come now, and let us reason together, saith the Lord; though your sins be as scarlet, they shall be as white as snow; though they be red like crimson, they shall be as wool."

Here are repentance and amendment of life and pardon, the washing away of guilt and committed sins, symbolical of the New Testament washing of regeneration, symbolical also of John's baptism of repentance unto the remission of sins.

But now in the sixth chapter, and "in the year that king Uzziah died," a wondrous vision of the pre-existent Christ, "sitting upon a throne high and lifted up" and the seraphim crying one to another "Holy, holy, holy is the Lord of hosts," was vouchsafed to the prophet. And the first effect of the glorious things which he saw and heard was not to exalt him and minister to his pride, but to fill him with despair at his own depravity. He felt just as Peter did at the first miraculous draught of fishes on the Sea of Galilee, when he exclaimed "Depart from me for I am a sinful man, O Lord." Ah! beloved, it never fosters spiritual pride, nor any other kind of pride to get a nearer and clearer view of Christ than we ever had before. Quite the contrary. Such a vision turns us towards our inner selves, and enables us to behold by contrast the darkness and sinfulness and pollution of our own souls, and in such a view we shall find food for the deepest humiliation, but nothing to nourish pride.

Accordingly, Isaiah exclaimed in agony of soul "Woe

is me! for I am undone; because I am a man of unclean lips, and I dwell in the midst of a people of unclean lips; for mine eyes have seen the King, the Lord of hosts." If we may credit Jewish tradition, it was for the offence of saying that he had seen the King, the Lord of hosts, that the prophet was afterwards sawn asunder. But the record of the glorious vision is still preserved and will, no doubt, be blessed to millions of readers in the future, as in the past, and until the end of the age.

But the seraph was sent to touch the "unclean lips" of Isaiah - unclean because of innate depravity, and unclean notwithstanding he had probably been preaching repentance and amendment of life and forgiveness for two or three years before this wondrous experience - to touch them with holy fire. And then he was assured not that his sins of commission and omission were forgiven - that had been done before – but that his iniquity was taken away, and his (inbred) sin purged. This was a second and a definite experience, and strikingly emblematic of the baptism with the Holy Ghost and fire under the gospel dispensation, which is also accompanied by "the purifying of the heart by faith," or entire sanctification.

How wondrous are the prophecies of Isaiah after this experience. He seems to look down the centuries for seven hundred years and to see the glorious blessings of the gospel dispensation almost as clearly as if they were already present. Hear him in the thirty-fifth chapter: "And an highway shall be there and a way; and it shall be called the way of holiness; the unclean shall not pass over it; but it shall be for those: the wayfaring men, though fools, shall not err therein." And in the fifty-first chapter: "Awake, awake! Put on thy strength, O Zion! put on thy beautiful garments, O

Jerusalem, the holy city; for henceforth, there shall no more come into thee the uncircumcised and the unclean," and in the sixtieth chapter: "Thy sun shall no more go down, neither shall thy moon withdraw itself; for the Lord shall be thine everlasting light, and the days of thy mourning shall be ended."

To Jeremiah the Lord said, "I sanctified thee; and I ordained thee a prophet unto the nations," which must mean not only that he was set apart for the office of a prophet, but also that he was cleansed from inbred sin, as a necessary preparation for the office itself.

In the thirty-sixth chapter of Ezekiel we have some striking passages on the theme before us. These were, no doubt, addressed primarily to the outward Israel, but they may very justly be appropriated by the Israel of God, the Church of Christ, since as Augustine says, "The New Testament lies hidden in the Old, and the Old is revealed in the New."

In the twenty-fifth verse we have the promise of pardon or justification with cleansing from the pollution of their past sins: "Then will I sprinkle clean water upon you and ye shall be clean, from all your filthiness and from all your idols will I cleanse you." Committed sin implies both guilt and pollution. And the pollution that is thus acquired by the practice of sinning is removed in regeneration. Thus the new convert is brought back again to the state of the little child. "Except ye be converted," said the blessed Saviour, "and become as little children, ye cannot enter into the kingdom of God." The little child has neither the guilt nor the pollution of committed sin; whilst he does have within him the inherited or inbred sin of his nature.

Now in the promise quoted above, allusion is made to the clean water made from the ashes of a red heifer and sprinkled, under the Mosaic law, upon those who had incurred ceremonial uncleanness. The thing signified, however, is the precious blood of Christ which cleanseth from all sin, or possibly the cleansing operation of the Holy Spirit, typified by water, may here be meant. At any rate the twenty-fifth verse points to nothing less than a full and free justification.

But the prophet continues: "A new heart also will I give you and a new spirit will I put within you; and I will take away the stony heart out of your flesh and I will give you a heart of flesh." Here we have described certainly the experience of regeneration, if indeed not the still fuller experience of entire sanctification. But let us admit that it means only the new heart which is given to the penitent sinner at his new birth. Regeneration implies the impartation of a new life by the Divine energy of the Holy Ghost. And this new life is comparable to the "heart of flesh," not, of course, a carnal heart, but a heart tender and teachable, and impressible to heavenly influences, such a heart as we always find in the new-born babe in Christ.

But listen still further: "And I will put My Spirit within you, and cause you to walk in My statutes, and ye shall keep My judgments and do them." In this verse we have a pre-figuring of the Holy Ghost baptism, by which the heart is cleansed from all sin and sanctified wholly, and also of the subsequent "walking in the Spirit," to which Paul alludes in one of his epistles. Zacharias, the father of John the Baptist, who was also seized with prophetic fire at the birth of his son, exclaims, "That He would grant unto us that we, being delivered out of the hand of our enemies, might serve

Him without fear, in holiness and righteousness before Him, all the days of our life." Surely the gospel of Christ has something better for its recipients than a constant daily sinning and repenting, which is too often the experience of Christian people. The twenty-seventh verse, therefore, signifies holiness of heart and life through the power of the indwelling Spirit.

How blessed it is thus to be assured that what we cannot do by our own strength, the Holy Spirit will cause us to do. This doctrine of spiritual causation is indeed glorious. Like the mainspring of the watch which supplies the power within, by which the hands are moved without, and thus the fleeting minutes and hours are correctly measured, so the Holy Spirit within supplies the energy by which the sanctified believer is enabled or caused to adorn the doctrine of Christ, his Saviour, in all things, and to bring forth the fruit of the Spirit in all righteousness and goodness and truth.

In the minor prophets, we find numerous allusions to the subject of holiness, though their language is often highly figurative. In Hosea 2:16, after reproving Israel for her unfaithfulness in the past, the Almighty, through His prophet, employs the following language, viz: "And it shall be at that day, saith the Lord, that thou shalt call Me Ishi, and shalt call Me no more Baali," and again in the nineteenth verse, "I will betroth thee unto Me forever; yea I will betroth thee in righteousness and in judgment and in loving kindness and in mercies; I will even betroth thee unto Me in faithfulness; and thou shalt know the Lord." Now the word Ishi means my husband; while the word Baali means my Lord, and the language, therefore, points to an experience or a relation of marriage. The bride is exalted immeasurably above the servant. While the position of the servant points to a legal justification and a service for wages and reward, that of the bride must signify entire sanctification, and the closest possible union with the Heavenly Bridegroom. Again, the word betrothed points legitimately to a marriage which is always justly expected to follow if both parties are faithful to the engagement. Beloved, let us get so near to Christ that we shall not address Him as my Lord, in the spirit of a servant, but as my husband, in the spirit of a loving and faithful wife. At your conversion, you are, as it were, betrothed to Him, or in ordinary language engaged to Him. At your entire sanctification, your engagement is consummated by the marriage union. Engagement must precede marriage, it is true, but, as a rule, engagements should not be long. Do not needlessly defer your nuptials, but rather hasten to the embraces of Everlasting Love. Like Rebecca, appreciate your high and holy calling, and like her say promptly and decidedly, "I will go."

In the book of Joel we find the prophecy which Peter quoted on the day of Pentecost, and assured the multitude of Jews, out of every nation under heaven, that what they beheld on that day was the fulfillment of the same. "And it shall come to pass afterward, that I will pour out My Spirit upon all flesh; and your sons and your daughters shall prophesy, your old men shall dream dreams, your young men shall see visions. And also upon the servants and upon the handmaidens in those days will I pour out My Spirit."

Now, these words are clearly a foreshadowing of the baptism with the Holy Ghost and fire, designed for all of God's children without distinction of nation or sex, and intended, first, to purify their hearts by faith (see Acts 15:9) and, secondly, to endue them with power for whatever line of service God may call them to. And we may add that this text, as well as many others, shows that in these gospel days women as well as men may be, as we find in the facts of our daily experience that they are both called and qualified for the work of the ministry, as well as other labors in the vineyard of the Lord. But both men and women need the Holy Ghost baptism which consumes inbred sin, as an indispensable qualification for the highest efficiency and most marked success in the work to which they may individually be called. Every Christian may and should do something for the Lord, but none can do all for Him which he makes it his privilege and his duty to do, without the grace of entire sanctification and the fulness of the Spirit.

In the prayer of Habakkuk we have some sentences which point unmistakably to the experience of perfect trust in God and perfect love for Him. "Although the fig-tree shall not blossom, neither shall fruit be in the vines; the labor of the olive shall fail, and the fields shall yield no meat; the flock shall be cut off from the fold, and there shall be no herd in the stalls; yet I will rejoice in the Lord, I will joy in the God of my salvation." Compare this with John Wesley's description of a holy man after Paul. One who is enabled to rejoice evermore, to pray without ceasing, and in everything to give thanks. Does not Habakkuk answer beautifully to this description?

The prophecy of Zechariah contains a number of visions, which are, no doubt, full of instruction to those who have eyes to see. We can only mention one or two of these. In the third chapter, verses one to seven, we are introduced to Joshua, the high priest, representing the Jewish people, and typifying Christ Jesus with His eternal and unchangeable priesthood after the order of Melchizedek. But the Angel Jehovah also represents Jesus in His capacity of Judge. And Satan, the adversary, is present as the accuser of the brethren, resisting them in the person of their representative, the high priest.

And surely it would seem, at first, as if there was ground for his accusations, for Joshua, the high priest, is clothed in filthy garments, and these can signify nothing else than sins, aye, the sins of His people imputed to Him as their representative and priest, and not their actual sins only but their inbred sin also, for, "The Lord hath laid on Him the iniquity of us all," and "He hath made Him to be sin for us who knew no sin." "His visage was so marred more than any man, and His form more than the sons of men." "He hath no form nor comeliness, and when we shall see Him, there is no beauty that we should desire Him."

"Many were astonished at thee," says Isaiah. "Behold the man," said Pilate, as he brought forth Jesus scourged, tortured, bleeding, but uncomplaining, and the only answer was "Crucify Him!" Thus, beloved, was He clothed in very truth with the filthy garments not of His own vileness but of ours.

But Joshua was "a brand plucked from the burning," and, therefore, in Him all His people have found pardon. And now comes the order "Take away the filthy garments from him, and unto him he said, Behold, I have caused thine iniquity to pass from thee, and I will clothe thee with change of raiment." Surely, beloved, we here have nothing less than entire sanctification, not in ourselves but in Him, and not only simply imputatively and representatively, but actually and experimentally. Praise the Lord.

The prophet Malachi assures us that "He shall sit as a refiner and purifier of silver; and He shall purify the sons of Levi" (that is, the "royal priesthood" which constitutes the true church) "and purge them as gold and silver, that they may offer unto the Lord an offering in righteousness." Surely no one will deny that there is holiness in prophecy.

CHAPTER VI.

ENTIRE SANCTIFICATION AS TAUGHT BY JESUS CHRIST.

Gabriel said to Mary in the annunciation, "Therefore, that holy thing that shall be born of thee shall be called the Son of God." Or in the Revised Version, "Wherefore, also, that which is to be born shall be called holy, the Son of God." The author of the Epistle to the Hebrews speaks of Him as "holy, harmless, undefiled, separate from sinners," and Peter says that "He did no sin, neither was guile found in His mouth." He is called "Thy holy child Jesus." Jesus Christ, therefore, was wholly free both from sin committed and sin indwelling. He was absolutely holy in heart and holy in life, holy in word and holy in act, holy in His birth, holy in His death, holy in His resurrection, holy in His ascension, holy in His eternity. Glory be to His Holy Name.

And if the Divine Founder of the Christian Church was thus a holy man, it would, naturally, be expected that He should desire to have a holy people; and if He desire it, that He should also make provision for it; and if He both desire it and hath made provision for it, that we should find allusions to it in His teachings. In this, we are not disappointed, as we shall proceed to show.

The Sermon on the Mount contains an epitome of the public preaching of the Lord Jesus, and every sentence is pregnant with meaning. From beginning to end, it inculcates holiness as the privilege and duty of believers. Many things are enjoined which would only be possible to those who are sanctified wholly, such as, "Bless them that curse you, do good to them that hate you, love your enemies, resist not evil," and many others.

The teachings of our Lord are like the headings of chapters, which are filled out and developed in the writings of the apostles. This is remarkably true of the Sermon on the Mount, which, without going largely into details, sets forth the principles which are to govern His kingdom on earth. The application and interpretation of these principles, He leaves to the inspired apostles and evangelists, who continued to teach and preach after His departure, and to the Holy Spirit who is promised to the believing church as its guide, teacher and comforter until Christ Himself shall come again.

But besides many precepts and injunctions which imply holiness, there are several, also, which expressly require it. Among the beatitudes at the beginning of the Sermon, we find this striking statement: "Blessed are the pure in heart for they shall see God." Now, heart purity cannot exist while there is any sin in the heart. Wherever there is sin in the heart, whether actual or indwelling, there is also defilement; and purity and defilement are incompatible terms.

Heart purity, therefore, is identical with entire sanctification, and heart purity is not only a great energizer, so that a man is powerful for good in proportion to the purity of his heart and life, but it is also a great illuminator, so that it enables its possessor to see God. This, of course, does not imply an open or an outward vision, but a spiritual apprehension of God, whereby we are brought into fellowship and communion with Him, and in a spiritual sense, we maybe truly regarded as seeing Him who is forever invisible to outward sense.

This inward purity, as distinguished from a blameless outward walk, was by no means unknown to the Old Testament writers. In the Twenty-fourth Psalm, David asks the question "Who shall ascend into the hill of the Lord? or who shall stand in His holy place?" And He immediately answers it by saying, "He that hath clean hands and a pure heart." The clean hands imply that his works are in accordance with God's law; in other words, that his outward life is free from condemnation. But the "pure heart" means more than this, and suggests what the same royal Psalmist remarks again in the Fifty-first Psalm. "Behold, thou desirest truth in the inward parts, in the hidden part, Thou shalt make me to know wisdom." It is also noticeable in the Twenty-fourth Psalm, as already quoted, that the clean hands or justification comes before the pure heart or entire sanctification. So accurate is the blessed spiritual logic of the Holy Ghost.

Returning to the Sermon on the Mount, we find at the end of Matthew fifth the direct command, "Be ye, therefore, perfect, even as your Father which is in heaven is perfect," or if we take the Revised Version, which is more accurate in translation, the command becomes a positive assertion, which is equally forcible. "Ye, therefore, shall be perfect as your Heavenly Father is perfect."

But whether command or declaration, it is at first sight simply astounding. It is overwhelming. So much so, indeed, that our poor human spirits shrink back in amazement, and we are ready to say, This is wholly impossible. Surely, Jesus cannot mean what He says. Or if He does, then my case is hopeless. But let us examine the words a little more carefully.

In the first place, we are to notice that He does not say that we are to be equal in perfection to our Father in Heaven. That would, indeed, be too absurd for the wildest fancy to conceive. God is infinite in all His attributes and, therefore, infinite in perfection, and this in all directions. We are poor, finite, sinful human beings, and can never even approach the boundless perfection of Him who is wholly without limit, either as to power, space or duration, or righteousness, justice and holiness.

But the command is not, Be ye equal to your Heavenly Father in perfection, but, Be ye perfect with the same kind of perfection which appertains to Him. It may be similar in kind whilst falling infinitely short of His perfection in degree. Now, God is infinite and perfect in all His attributes, but apart from His attributes is His essence. And what is the perfection which is predicated of the essence of God? Or, rather, what is His essence itself? It is love. "God is love," says the apostle. "Thy nature and Thy name is love," says the great hymnologist, Charles Wesley. The essential perfection of the Godhead, therefore, is a perfection of love. And we are assured by the beloved John that it is possible for us, also, to be made perfect in love, and to possess the perfect love which casteth out fear. Hence, if we are perfect in love we are perfect even as our Father who is in heaven is perfect. Behold the blessed simplicity of the gospel.

The context of the command referred to proves the same thing. Jesus had just been telling His disciples that it is not sufficient for them to love their friends, and do good to those that do good to them. All these things and more are done even by worldly minded people and open sinners. Unsaved people love those who love them. But Jesus continues, "I say unto you, love your enemies; bless them that curse you; do good to them that hate you, and pray for them that despitefully use you and persecute you." Why? "That ye may be the children of your Father who is in heaven," for that is just the way He does. He does not wait for a man to be His friend before He loves him and shows kindness to him. "He maketh His sun to rise on the evil and on the good, and sendeth rain on the just and on the unjust." And, if we are to be the children of such a Father, we must adopt His sentiments and love in our measure as He loves. His essence being love, all His infinite activities are controlled and regulated and directed by love, and when there is nothing contrary to love in our hearts, so that all our finite activities are in like manner impelled and swayed and directed by love, then we are perfect in love, and perfect even as our Heavenly Father is perfect. Glory to His Name.

I believe that if we search carefully and prayerfully we shall find the doctrine of entire sanctification in many of the parables of our Saviour. Take, for instance, the parable of the sower. Here we are expressly told that the seed is the word of God, and, of course, the sowers are all ministers and Christian workers who are trying in any right way, to diffuse a knowledge and acceptance of gospel truth. They are devoting themselves to the salvation of human souls. Now, mark the difference as to the ground upon which the good seed falls. (1) The wayside hearers are not concerted at all. (2) The stony ground hearers are converted but not established. Their shallowness is such as to prevent them from withstanding trial and temptation and hence they fall into backsliding. (3) The thorny ground hearers are converted, but inbred sin remains in their hearts in form of the love of riches, whether these riches are possessed or only desired, or too much care and cumber, having so much regard to the secular as to neglect the spiritual, or in the form of unsanctified desire, "the lusts of other things," and so by sin that dwelleth in them the word is "choked," and though they may bring forth a little meagre fruit of inferior quality, yet they bring "no fruit to perfection." They are justified but not sanctified wholly.

Now, our Heavenly Father desires not a little fruit but much fruit. "Every branch that bringeth forth fruit, he purgeth it that it may bring forth more fruit." To purge is to purify or, in a spiritual sense, to sanctify, and this is the condition of abundant fruitage. When the thorns are removed the good seed will grow and flourish. When inbred sin is taken out of the heart the Christian believer will bring forth fruit to perfection, even the perfection of love, and this will be the "much fruit" whereby God is glorified.

On one occasion we are told that a lawyer asked Jesus "What shall I do to inherit eternal life?" and when asked in reply what were the words of the Mosaic law he answered, "Thou shalt love the Lord thy God with all thy heart and with all thy soul and with all thy mind; and thy neighbor as thyself." Jesus commended his answer and added "This do and thou shalt live."

Hence, our Saviour teaches that holiness consists of nothing more nor less nor else than perfect love to God and man. What constitutes this love has been already explained.

Martha was a good Christian, but she was "careful and troubled about many things." Mary was a good Christian and still earnestly seeking the one thing needful, which is full salvation, or holiness of heart and life. Even good Christians may be "cumbered about much serving," and so miss this one thing needful. We cannot doubt that both the sisters, who vividly typify the two experiences, obtained the blessing of holiness when the pentecostal baptism was poured out upon the church of the hundred and twenty, if not before. In the marvelous intercessory prayer of the Lord Jesus, given in the seventeenth of John, we find these expressions, "Sanctify them through Thy truth. Thy word is truth." And again, "For their sakes I sanctify Myself that they also may be sanctified through the truth." Here we discover the two senses of the word sanctify. Jesus sets Himself apart or consecrates Himself to the work of human redemption in order that His followers, in all ages, may be not only set apart or consecrated, but also sanctified wholly, or made holy in heart and life. He gave Himself for the world of sinners lost, that they might be forgiven and saved. He gave Himself for the church, on the other hand, that He might "sanctify and cleanse it with the washing of water by the word, that He might present it to Himself a glorious church, not having spot nor wrinkle nor any such thing, but that it should be holy and without blemish." Thus, the atoning sacrifice of Christ procured pardon and acceptance for the penitent sinner. It procured not less, certainly, entire sanctification for the consecrated believer. And it is only by accepting Him as a perfect Saviour that He "is made of God unto us, wisdom and righteousness and sanctification and redemption."

For the blessed Saviour does not leave us in doubt as to the method of obtaining this great blessing of holiness, nor as to the price, which must be paid for it. Entire sanctification is "one pearl of great price," and he who would possess it must go and sell all that he has. The rich young ruler had a first-class record as to morality and the outward observance of the law of God, yet Jesus said to him, "One thing thou lackest," and that one thing was perfect love, for He added, "If thou wilt be perfect, go and sell that thou hast and give to the poor," and then interjecting a promise, "Thou shalt have treasure in heaven, and come take up the cross and follow Me." The price was too great, and the young man went away sorrowful. Alas! Myriads of souls since have found the price too great, and by refusing to pay it, have deprived themselves of unspeakable blessing. Christ would not have us become His followers without counting the cost, and the cost is all that we have and all that we are. "Whosoever forsaketh not all that he hath, he cannot be My disciple."

First, we are to forsake, with full purpose of heart, all known sin. It may be the sin which "easily besets," our own bosom sin, near as a right eye or a right hand, but if it causes us to stumble, it must be relentlessly sacrificed. And even if the sacrifice seems like crippling and maiming us, yet Jesus assures us that it is better to enter into eternal life with one eye or one hand, than to be consigned to everlasting death with two eyes or two hands. In the first place, therefore, we are to "reckon ourselves dead, indeed, unto sin, but alive unto God through Jesus Christ, our Lord."

But we are to become dead, indeed, not only to all sin, but we must be dead, also, even to lawful things, except as God in His mercy may grant them to us, to have and enjoy in moderation and to His glory. Jesus teaches us that our highest affection, our deepest love must be fastened upon Him alone, and that if any individual love, father or mother, son or daughter, wife or husband more than Him, such a one is not worthy of Him. We are to love His gifts and thank Him for them, but still more are we to love the Giver Himself.

And when we love Him supremely, we shall learn to be satisfied with Himself, and what He in His love and mercy chooses to give us. If He permits us to have an abundance of earthly goods, we shall thank Him and use them as stewards of His for His glory. If He allows our family circle to be invaded by death, and one dear one after another is carried away to the tomb, or if He permits our wealth to be taken from us and consign us to poverty and desolation, if His gifts one by one or altogether are withdrawn from us, why, praise the Lord, we still have the Giver, and can still say with Job "The Lord gave and the Lord hath taken away. Blessed be the name of the Lord."

It thus appears that the teachings of our Lord require us to be dead to sin, and dead to self, yea, even to lawful self, in order that we may possess this inestimable blessing of entire sanctification. Let us not hesitate, then, beloved, to lay down our lives. "Whosoever will save his life shall lose it, but whosoever will lose his life for My sake, the same shall save it."

"Except a corn of wheat fall into the ground and die, it abideth alone; but if it die, it bringeth forth much fruit."

CHAPTER VII.

ENTIRE SANCTIFICATION AS TAUGHT BY PAUL.

The apostleship of the Gentiles was committed specially to Paul. And as the Gospel of Christ is intended for the salvation not of the Jews only, but of all mankind who are willing to accept the conditions, we find in the writings of this apostle, perhaps, a more complete exposition and expansion of the teachings of the Lord Jesus than in any other inspired author. Jesus gave the concise germinal principles of all gospel truth; and Paul deduces from these principles their logical consequences and develops them, under the inspiration of the Holy Spirit, into those wonderful epistles to the churches, which, though as Peter well observes containing some things hard to be under-stood, are no doubt destined, nevertheless, in the future as in the past, to form a large part both of the foundation and framework of every system of theological doctrine. How wondrous, for instance, is the scheme of redemption as unfolded to us in the Epistle to the Romans! How profound and how exalted is the spirituality of the Ephesians and Colossians! How pure and how practical are the directions to the Corinthians! What a counter-blast to all legality in the church do we have in Galatians! What a marvelous unfolding of Old Testament typology in the Hebrews!

What a guidebook of unequalled excellency for ministers of all times in the pastoral epistles!

In the Epistle to the Romans, Paul regards mankind under the two divisions of the Gentile and the Jew, and proceeds to show that both classes alike had failed in their efforts to attain to righteousness and salvation.

The Gentile, it is true, had not been favored with an outward revelation, but he had been permitted to behold the outward universe, and to know that it had a Creator "of eternal power and divinity." He had also had a conscience within him, and so much light as rendered him an accountable being, with a sense of obligation to a supreme power, and furnishing another proof of the existence of a personal God. But the Apostle tells us that they, the Gentiles, did not like to retain God in their knowledge. They wickedly extinguished the light which He had given them, because they were not willing to give up their immoralities. And as their hearts became more corrupt, their intellects also were darkened, and in their senselessness they changed the glory of the incorruptible God into the baser image of "birds and four-footed beasts and creeping things." They sank into the grossest idolatry and licentiousness and all wickedness. This picture drawn in colors which shock our sensibilities, in the first chapter of Romans, is confirmed by the authentic writings of heathen historians, and this in all particulars, Paul says, "They are without excuse, because they did not live up to the light which they had received, obscure and imperfect as it was."

And how was it with the Jews? The advantage was, indeed, to them much every way, but chiefly because to them were committed the oracles of God. They had an outward revelation, and with it a knowledge of that law of God, which is holy and just and good.

But they had failed, if possible, more grievously than the Gentiles themselves. They had received the law by the disposition of angels, as Stephen told them and had not kept it. They had had far more light than the Gentiles, but they had fallen into the same sins as they. They prided themselves on the law, and looked with contempt upon the Gentiles, and condemned them for their immoralities, and yet were guilty of similar immoralities themselves. They talked loudly about the words of the law. "Do not steal." "Do not commit adultery," and yet violated these very commands themselves. Jesus in His scathing denunciation of the Scribes and Pharisees, compared them to whited sepulchres, looking well outwardly, but within full of dead men's bones and all uncleanness: and He warned His disciples to beware of the leaven of the Pharisees, which is hypocrisy, and the leaven of the Sadduces, which is infidelity, and the leaven of the Herodians, which is worldly mindedness.

The cause of failure was the same, both with Jew and Gentile. It was something that had occurred long before the division into Jew and Gentile had an existence. It had occurred, in short, when man fell. From fallen parents our entire race had inherited a fallen nature, that is to say, a natural proclivity towards sin. There is a disposition in all mankind to yield to temptation, some in one direction, some in another, and thus to say yes to Satan, while they also say no to God. This bias towards evil is sometimes called depravity or original sin. It is called by Paul "Our old man," "the flesh," "the carnal mind," "the body of sin," and "sin that dwelleth in me." A good and convenient name for it is inbred sin. It is sin in the heart as distinguished from sin in the act. It is the inward cause of which our outward sins are the effects. It is the evil root of which our outward sins are the bitter fruits.

Now, it was the inbred sin in the hearts of the Gentiles which caused them to quench the light of the knowledge of God, which they must have had for, at least, a generation or two after Noah came out of the ark, and which made them blind to the light even of natural religion, notwithstanding before their eyes the heavens were declaring the glory of God and the firmament was showing His handiwork, day unto day was uttering speech, and night unto night was showing knowledge. They forsook the knowledge of God, and He left them to their own reprobate minds, the result being that they sank into the grossest idolatry and the most beastly sensuality.

The Jew had the unspeakable advantage of an outward revelation. He received through Moses the law of God, which showed him what God desired him to be and do, and what he ought to be and do, but which conferred upon him no power for being or doing what it required. It is like a looking-glass placed before a child to show him that his face is soiled, but having no power to cleanse that face. It was like a plumb-line applied to a leaning wall, which shows how far it deviates from the perpendicular, but which has no power to make it upright. Nay, it even comes to pass that in consequence of inbred sin, the law multiplies offences. It causes sin to abound. We find even in most children a disposition that impels them to do and to have just what they are told they must not do and have. That is to say, when the law comes in, inbred sin rises in rebellion against it.

The workings of the sin that dwelleth in us is most vividly described by Paul in the seventh chapter of Romans. Over the real meaning of this chapter, there has been much discussion and wide differences of opinion. Some writers think that this is the best experience of the great apostle of the Gentiles, and they draw consolation from this fact, as well as argument, in favor of continuing to sin in thought and word and deed as long as they live. Others think that the apostle is not here describing a Christian experience at all, but the struggles of a Jew who is seeking the favor of God by keeping His law, but finds his attempts to keep it all in vain, the hindrance being inbred sin. I freely admit that it is not what even a justified experience ought to be, for God has assured us through His apostle, John, that He that is born of God doth not commit sin, and, therefore, notwith-standing the presence of inbred sin in the heart of the justified and regenerated believer, yet such a one, by watchfulness and prayer, may be kept from acts of sin and from becoming a backslider. But in point of fact, the seventh of Romans does describe what, in many cases, is the experience of the converted Christian.

For there are many who even after a clear conversion and a joyful sense of God's favor, with the witness of the Spirit to their adoption, yet do yield to temptation under the pressure of inbred sin, and so pass weeks, or months or weary years in what is called an up-and-down experience, not becoming confirmed backsliders, but sinning and repenting, delighting in the law of God after the inward man, but often yielding to the demands of the law of sin, which is in their members, not losing their sonship, but losing their communion and their joy, often like Peter weeping bitterly over their transgressions, but finding that while the spirit is willing, the flesh is weak.

I said that such a process, unsatisfactory as it is, might go on for years. It ends either in complete religious declension amounting, sometimes, to apostacy on the one hand, or infinitely better, in the entire sanctification of the heart and complete deliverance from inbred sin. And in these days of enlightenment, when the doctrine and experience of holiness are so plainly taught, and so generally diffused among the children of God, it is, at least, doubtful whether a soul can continue long in a state of justification, which means that it will either go forward to the experience of entire sanctification, or else it will fall into back-sliding as did some of the Corinthians, or into legality as did the Galatians.

Now, legality is nothing more nor less than Judaism. It is seeking salvation after the pattern of the Old Testament, and not after that of the New. It is a matter of works, and not a matter of faith. It inquires "What good thing shall I do that I may inherit eternal life?" It is the child of the bondwoman and not that of the free. It is Ishmael and not Isaac. It is Sinai and not Calvary.

And so it happens that many Christians are simply good Jews. They may even possess circumcised hearts, and may yet serve the Lord in the spirit of bondage, as did good Jews of old. They fail to realize that they have been called unto liberty, which liberty does not, by any means, signify license; it does not signify the liberty of making our own choices, but the liberty of accepting gladly and submissively God's choices; it does not mean the liberty of doing either right or wrong as we may prefer, but the liberty of always preferring to do right and never wrong, and so to spend our years on earth, doing right in all directions, and doing wrong in none. This, beloved, is the glorious liberty of the children of God.

After the birth of Ishmael, we may well suppose that Hagar's chief employment in Abraham's house was to look after the said Ishmael, to care for him and to restrain him. Mark, it was never her business to care for or to restrain Isaac. He was the child of promise, the child of faith, the son of the lawful wife and the free woman, and when Ishmael's persecuting spirit broke forth at the weaning of Isaac, then the command was "Cast out the bond woman and her son." Both must go together or stay together. Ah! beloved, when inbred sin is cast out, there is no more need of the law either to restrain or constrain. Perfect love casts out fear; it also casts out sin, and becomes the motive power of the whole spiritual man. "The love of Christ constraineth us."

So Paul shows us that both Gentiles and Jews had failed to attain unto the law of righteousness, because of inbred sin, which caused the former to put out the light which they had, and the latter to fall short of keeping the law, which was their only hope of salvation, but which was never intended by its Divine Author to save men, but to show them how utterly incapable they were of saving themselves.

But Paul does not leave them there. After putting both classes of the human family into the same position of failure and condemnation, and declaring that there is no difference, "for all have sinned and come short of the glory of God," he adds, "Being justified fully by His grace, through the redemption that is in Christ Jesus." When man's helplessness and inability have been sufficiently demonstrated, then God comes to his rescue. "For God hath concluded them all in unbelief, that He might have mercy upon all."

Thus in the Epistle to the Romans, the apostle teaches the great doctrine of justification by faith and the consequent peace of reconciliation, the "peace with God through our Lord Jesus Christ." But he goes farther than justification, and shows us that sanctification, also, is by faith and not by works. He will not be satisfied with anything less than the death of our old man, and the death of inbred sin is precisely the experience of entire sanctification. "Knowing this that our old man is crucified with him, that the body of sin might be destroyed, that, henceforth, we should not serve him."

But we are wholly unable to destroy or do away with the body of sin by any resolution or will-power or effort of our own. Sin will not go dead at our bidding, nor can we become dead to sin by wishing or striving to be so. Again, we are brought face to face with our helplessness, but the apostle solves the problem for us by directing us to resort to the process of reckoning. "Likewise reckon ye, also, yourselves to be dead, indeed, unto sin, but alive unto God, through Jesus Christ, our Lord." Ah! now, our help is laid upon one that is mighty. "The things that are impossible with men are possible with God." What we reckon, with the sublime reckoning of faith, Christ can make real and true. We have only, therefore, to reckon ourselves to be dead, indeed, unto sin, and leave to Him to make the reckoning good. But we must not fail to reckon ourselves alive as well as dead. And to be alive to God means, in this connection, to be responsive to every intimation of His will, to love Him perfectly, to be, to do and to suffer joyfully all that He may determine concerning us, in short, to be sanctified wholly. Oh, beloved, what a blessed reckoning is the reckoning of faith! How vastly does it transcend all the reckonings of logic or mathematics. For, by it, we experience a continual deadness to sin, and a continual holiness of heart and life.

For it must be clearly understood that Paul is not asking us to fancy, or imagine, or hypothecate. He is not telling us that if we believe a thing to be true, the believing will make it true. He is not persuading us to reckon without factors and with no result. The factors in his direction are God's promises and commands, alike in the Old Testament and in the New, urging His people to be holy, and promising to make them so, and our acceptance of the provision He has made for our cleansing, by faith, and then by the reckoning alluded to, the result is secured.

In foggy or cloudy weather, mariners at sea are often compelled to resort to what they term dead-reckoning. Sometimes for days together, the sun is hidden by clouds, and no observation can be taken with the usual instruments for determining latitude and longitude. Then the captain ascertains by the compass what direction he is pursuing, and by the log, the rate at which the ship is sailing, and thus by marking out his daily advance on a chart, he is enabled, with astonishing accuracy, to determine when and at what point he will sight the shore toward which the voyage is directed. What he reckons becomes real, when he tells the passengers, "Within five minutes, we ought to see the Irish coast," followed within the specified time by the cry from the lookout, "Land, ho!"

To the Christian believer, the Bible is both compass and log and chart. Sometimes, he enjoys the witness of the Spirit clear as the sunshine, assuring him that he is going in the right direction, and informing him as to his whereabouts in Christian experience, but when not thus favored, he can still move on by faith, he still has his compass and his chart, and he can still employ the dead-reckoning, and go forward with a holy trust that in due time he shall land in the heavenly port. Praise the Lord.

To comment in detail upon all that the great apostle of the Gentiles has written in reference to entire sanctification would require a volume instead of a single chapter. I must, therefore, content myself with a few selections, and leave the reader to pursue the subject for himself in the inexhaustible mine of the Pauline Epistles.

In Romans 6:13, we have the best description of consecration that is to be found anywhere. "Neither yield ye your members as instruments of unrighteousness unto sin; but yield yourselves unto God, as those that are alive from the dead, and your members as instruments of righteousness unto God." And, again, in the 19th verse, "For as ye have yielded your members servants to uncleanness and to iniquity, unto iniquity; even so, now, yield your members servants to righteousness, unto holiness."

Here, the apostle clearly teaches us that consecration is not the same thing as entire sanctification. The one is an act proceeding from man to God, the other is an act proceeding from God to man. It is man who consecrates; it is God who sanctifies.

Perfect consecration is an entire surrender of a personal human being to a personal God. The term members may well be understood to include all bodily organs and powers, all mental faculties and sensibilities, and all appurtenances, such as time, money, influence, culture, health, and, in short, the whole personal, individual man, with all his belongings. The surrender must be complete, absolute, unreserved and forever. Body, soul, spirit, time, talents, possessions, all that we have and all that we are must be His, wholly His, and His to all eternity.

Such a consecration cannot be made by any one who is not already a Christian believer. Paul informs us, explicitly, that he is not calling upon sinners "dead in trespasses and sins," to consecrate themselves, but upon converted persons, "those who are alive from the dead." How thankful we ought to be that he has settled that point forever. Sinners may repent, but only Christians can consecrate. Whatever surrender the sinner may and must make in order to be saved, the believer must make a broader, deeper, fuller, more complete surrender of a different character and for a different purpose. In repentance, the sinner gives himself away as a dead sacrifice, and his purpose is to receive pardon and life. In consecration, the Christian yields to God his living and regenerated faculties and powers, and his purpose is that he may be sanctified wholly, filled with the Spirit, and used to the utmost extent of his capacity for the glory of God.

Consecration does not mean the giving up of our sins, or vices, or depraved appetites, or forbidden indulgences. We cannot consecrate our alcohol, or our tobacco, or our opium, or our card-playing, or dancing, or theater-going to God. He wants none of these things.

All actual and known sins must be abandoned at conversion. Our consecration is for a deeper work, that is to say, for the removal of inbred sin, which, after all, is not accomplished by our consecration, though that is an essential preliminary, but by the baptism with the Holy Ghost and fire.

The essence of consecration is in the sentence, "Yield yourselves unto God." When you yield yourselves, you yield everything else. All the details are included in the one surrender of yourself. Changing the emphasis, we may read again, "Yield yourselves unto God." Consecration is not to God's service, not to His work, not to a life of obedience and sacrifice, not to the church, not to the Christian Endeavor, not to the missionary cause, nor even to the cause of God; it is to God Himself. "Yield yourselves unto God." Your work, your service, your obedience, your sacrifice, your right place and your allotted duty will all follow in good time.

Consecration is the willingness, and the resolution and the purpose to be, to do, and to suffer all God's will. Its essence, already given in the words of Paul, is given also in the words of the Saviour. "Not My will but Thine be, done," which is beautifully versified by Frances Ridley Havergal, in the couplet,

"Take my will and make it thine,
It shall be no longer mine."

Consecration being a definite transaction, and made once for all, does not need to be repeated unless we have failed to keep it. To consecrate over and over again is like a husband and wife marrying over and over again. We are consecrated just as we are married.

The vow is upon us, and in the force of that vow, we walk all our days. All we have to do is to remember day by day that we are wholly the Lord's, and see to it that nothing is taken from the altar. Those who have kept their consecration complete should testify to its maintenance upon all suitable occasions, and never deny it by word, deed or silence.

Many years ago, I saw a form of consecration in an English periodical, which is here given very slightly modified, and which has been adopted by many. Let all my readers unite with the author in entering into this personal yielding to God.

I am willing

To receive what Thou givest,
To lack what Thou withholdest,
To relinquish what Thou takest,
To suffer what Thou inflictest,
To be what Thou requirest,
To do what Thou commandest.

Amen.

In this connection, we may add that when the consecration is complete, it becomes, comparatively, an easy matter to believe. Entire sanctification like justification, and, indeed, all other gospel blessings and experiences, is to be received by faith. But so long as the surrender to God is not complete, faith refuses to act.

When all obstructions are removed by an act of heartfelt and sincere consecration, then it becomes as natural and as easy to believe as it is to breathe, after everything that hinders breathing is removed from the air passages. We hear much complaint among Christians of a want of faith. If they only had more faith, they imagine that all would be well. When the disciples of old asked Jesus to increase their faith, He told them, in effect, to use what they had. If it were only a mustard-seed faith, He assured them that it would remove mountains. And we may justly conclude that the difficulty with most seekers after entire sanctification is not in a want of faith so much as in an incomplete surrender. The carnal mind dies very hard. It attaches itself to one worldly thing or another, and refuses to be sundered from what it loves, and while this is the case, the individual cannot believe that God gives him the unspeakable blessing of heart purity. But when all the preliminaries have been attended to, and there is nothing else needed but to trust in Jesus, then faith can appropriate His promises, and in so doing realize their fulfillment.

Another class of seekers is very much concerned about the witness of the Spirit to assure them that the blessing has been received. Probably in these cases the very point that has not yet been consecrated to God is the feeling, or the witness, which they so much desire. "It often happens," says Dr. G. D. Watson, "that a patient, who has been cured of some contagious disease, has to have a certificate on leaving the hospital. In such a case the certificate does not cure him, but certifies that he is cured. How absurd for a patient just entering the hospital to clamor for his health certificate before receiving the doctor and taking the remedies. In like manner, it is useless for a seeking soul to be clamoring for the witness and waiting for the feeling before receiving Jesus and fully trusting Him for the cure. We are not to trust in the experience, but the Saviour who imparts the experience."

Let us now return to Paul. In his first epistle to the Corinthians, second and third chapters, he tells us of three classes of persons: the natural man, the spiritual man, and the babe in Christ. The natural man, he tells us, receiveth not the things of the Spirit of God; they are foolishness unto him; neither can he know them, because they are spiritually discerned. Such is a description of the unregenerate wherever and whenever they are found. Their standard of judgment is not that of the Holy Spirit. They are blind to the truth of God and deaf to the story of salvation. Being without spiritual life they are, of course, without spiritual judgment. And yet, just such persons are in all our churches, and the number is by no means small. And often it strangely happens that these are the very individuals who are noticeably forward in expressing their opinions on the right way of managing a church. Fine and costly edifices, artistic music, entertainments and theatricals, eloquent preaching or lecturing, something to be proud of and to draw the crowd - these are the things which in their view make the church of their choice a success; but as for the conversion of sinners, as for the spread of the gospel at home and abroad, as for the sanctifying of believers, as for the things of the Spirit of God, they are foolishness unto them. What they need is a deep and pungent conviction, a true repentance, a living faith and a sound conversion. May God hasten it in His time.

"He that is spiritual," says our apostle, "judgeth or discerneth all things, yet he himself is judged or discerned of no man." The spiritual man is the man who has been baptized with the Spirit and filled with the Spirit, and in whom the Spirit abides as an ever-present Guide, Comforter and Friend. In short, he is the man who is wholly sanctified and saved to the uttermost. I should not, of course, affirm that such a one is always remarkable for depth or soundness of judgment, for, as his religion is in his heart rather than in his head, the heart may be perfect while the head may be weak. And yet holiness, or rather the Holy Spirit dwelling in the heart, does have a wonderfully illuminating influence upon the understanding. And the spiritual man, however many things he may be ignorant of, does understand the condition of the natural man, because he has been there, while he is not understood by the natural man because the latter has not been where he is. And the same is true of the relation of the spiritual man to the carnal Christian or babe in Christ. He, also, is understood by one who has the Spirit, while he is himself incapable of judging or discerning the position of the latter.

Paul assures the Corinthians that they are "yet carnal," and still he asserts that they are "babes in Christ." Such persons, and their name is legion in all denominations of Christians, are not wholly natural, neither are they wholly spiritual. They are babes in Christ, and, there-fore, they may thank God that they are in Christ. They are converted, they are believers, they are disciples, they are justified; but they are not wholly sanctified, and not wholly delivered from the carnal mind. Their state is a mixed one, partly spiritual, partly carnal.

Oh, let such as these make an immediate and complete and irrevocable consecration to God, and let them ask for the baptism with the Holy Ghost and receive Him by faith in His sanctifying and empowering offices, that so they may become, not partly, but wholly spiritual. Oh, that spiritual men and women may increase and abound in all our churches. Amen.

In 2 Corinthians, 7:1, the apostle of the Gentiles bases the experience of entire sanctification on the glorious promises of God. "Having, therefore, these promises, dearly beloved, let us cleanse ourselves from all filthiness of the flesh and spirit, perfecting holiness in the fear of God." To cleanse ourselves is shown by the Greek tense to be an act done definitely and once for all. It means, therefore, to put ourselves under the conditions of cleansing by a definite act of consecration to God. It means to place ourselves in co-operation with the Holy Spirit, who is distinctively the Sanctifier and Cleanser. It means, also, that we are to seek and find the baptism with the Holy Ghost and with fire, in order that our hearts may be purified by faith, and then to continually avoid all sources of temptation and all incentives to evil, so far as we may; and continuously realize and experience the holiness which Christ has instantaneously wrought in our souls through His Holy Spirit. Filthiness of the flesh signifies undue indulgence of sensual appetites, as in gluttony, drunkenness and licentiousness, which was probably very prevalent at Corinth. Filthiness of the spirit is illustrated by idolatry and pride, nor must we forget that the spirit is often polluted also through pampering the body.

Paul's wonderful prayer in Ephesians 3:14-21, has been so admirably treated of by Dr. Daniel Steele, that I shall content myself with referring the reader to his book on "Love Enthroned," page 123, and pass on. A single remark, however, may properly be made. That prayer, undoubtedly, embodies all that we mean by entire sanctification and the filling of the Spirit and more.

In 1 Thess. 5:23, we have another prayer of the great apostle in which entire sanctification is expressly petitioned for. "And the very God of peace sanctify you wholly: and I pray God your whole spirit and soul and body be preserved blameless unto the coming of our Lord Jesus Christ. Faithful is he that calleth you, who also will do it." The very form of the expression in the first clause indicates that it is possible to be sanctified wholly and possible to be sanctified partially. All Christians are cleansed from the pollution of sins committed, that is to say, from the pollution they have acquired by actually sinning. And thus the Corinthians are addressed by Paul as sanctified, although, manifestly, many of them were not holy in heart and life. On the other hand, the apostle prays that the Thessalonians may be sanctified wholly, although as a church they were already in a healthy and prosperous condition, the only exception being a few members who were too neglectful of their outward business and too much disposed to be busy-bodies. So we may conclude, without hesitation, that all Christians are partially sanctified, while many good Christians are not wholly sanctified.

But provision was made in the gospel for the entire sanctification of all believers, otherwise Paul would not have prayed for it. And not only for their entire sanctification as a definite, instantaneous act of God, as shown by the Greek tense, but, also, for their continual preservation in blamelessness, though not in faultlessness, until the coming of our Lord Jesus Christ. And lest they should stagger through unbelief he adds, "Faithful is He that calleth you. You are not to do it. He will do it for He is able."

And this experience extends to the whole man, the

spirit which takes hold of and communes with God, the soul with its emotions, affections, desires and volitions; the body with its appetites and its powers all made holy and preserved holy. Glory!

One more citation only and I will leave the reader to his own researches in the rich storehouse of the Pauline writings. Taking it for granted that Paul is the author of the Hebrews, let us read chapter 7:25 of that profound epistle. "Wherefore, he is able, also, to save them to the uttermost that come unto God by Him, seeing He ever liveth to make intercession for them." To the uttermost refers, undoubtedly, not only to time but to quantity. It means entirely, perfectly, altogether, through and through. And if he is able he is also willing. Oh, that all my readers, with the writer, may praise God now and evermore for salvation from the uttermost to the uttermost. Amen.

CHAPTER VIII.

ENTIRE SANCTIFICATION AS TAUGHT
BY PETER.

In the first place, Peter sanctioned all the writings of his beloved brother, Paul, and this probably at a period when Paul was either dead or separated from his ministerial work by imprisonment. There is a tradition that both the apostles were put to death on the same day at Rome, the one by crucifixion, choosing himself to have his head downward because unworthy to die just like his Master - the other by beheading, because he was a Roman citizen, which was deemed, at Rome, too honorable a position to be subjected to the ignominious death of the cross. Even if this should be true, yet Peter's second epistle, in which he endorses Paul's teachings, and gives to his writings the same authority as to the rest of the Bible, seems to have been written but a short time previous to his own martyrdom. The mature judgment of Peter, therefore, was that Paul was an inspired writer of Scripture, and that what he had given to the churches through his epistles, and left as a permanent legacy for the church universal, is to be received as gospel truth. And this will apply to his copious and frequent allusions to entire sanctification, as well as to the various other subjects treated of by his inspired pen. On the subject of holiness, therefore, Peter and Paul are as one; and we need not be surprised that in the very first sentence of his first epistle, he addresses the Christians of the Jewish dispersion in Asia Minor - though by no means excluding the Gentile converts - as elect according to the fore-knowledge (not predestination) of God the Father through sanctification of the Spirit, which must include entire as well as partial sanctification, unto (not unconditional happiness or misery,) but unto obedience and sprinkling of the blood of Jesus Christ. Thus, in one grand outburst of salutation from his glowing heart, he associates sanctification of the Spirit, the blood of sprinkling, and the obedience of faith. Neither Peter nor Paul stops in the midst of his earnest appeals to men's hearts, in order to give a lecture on Systematic Theology, but both scatter seed-thoughts all over their inspired pages, which are abundant in fruitage to the candid and reflecting mind. And right here we remark that Paul to the Thessalonians employs the same expression, sanctification of the spirit, in connection with belief of the truth, and thus putting the apostle of the circumcision by the side of the apostle of the uncircumcision we have sanctification by the blood of Jesus, sanctification by faith, sanctification by the Holy Ghost, and even in a subordinate sense, sanctification by obedience, and all this without the slightest inconsistency or contradiction.

And as Peter starts out by calling God's people to holiness, he continues by reminding them that their hope is to be fixed upon "an inheritance incorruptible and undefiled and that fadeth not away, reserved in heaven for you." What more natural than that those who are expecting to inherit a holy heaven, should themselves seek while here to become a holy people? Surely we should desire a meetness for our inheritance as well as a title to it.

After speaking of the "trial of their faith being much more precious than of gold which perisheth," the apostle utters forth an imperious call to entire sanctification. "But as He which hath called you is holy, so be ye holy in all manner of conversation; because it is written, Be ye holy, for I am holy." Thus he quotes from the words of the great lawgiver in Leviticus - that Moses, whom all Jews have delighted to honor, and shows at a glance that the Old Testament, as well as the New, bears witness to the holiness of God, and makes that fact a sufficient reason for the command and requirement that His people should be holy, also.

Our Heavenly Father, then, is a holy God and dwells in a holy heaven. Is it not most reasonable and most fit that He should require all who are to dwell with Him forever in that holy place, to be holy also? And in order to find an abundant entrance into that everlasting kingdom, we must be made holy while still clothed in flesh and sojourning upon earth. Nothing that is not already pure and holy can pass through the gates of pearl into the eternal city, the New Jerusalem.

Holiness is what constitutes the family likeness between our Father in heaven and His children both on earth and in heaven. A lady was accosted in the streets of a western city by a stranger, who asked her if she was not the daughter of such a one, naming him. She replied, with some surprise at the question, in the affirmative. "I knew you," said the gentleman, "by your resemblance to your father who was my particular friend twenty-five years ago, away back in the State of Maine." And the lady was delighted that the lineaments of her father's countenance were so impressed upon her own that she should thus be recognized even by one who had never seen her before as her father's child.

Ah! beloved, have we the likeness of our Heavenly Father so imprinted upon our faces and upon our walk and upon our conversation that all who know Him shall recognize His features in us? Oh, for more of the family likeness which shall stamp us as sons of God wherever we are and whatever we do. "Be ye holy, for I am holy."

In comparison with the precious "blood of Christ" Peter characterizes silver and gold, which men call precious metals, as "corruptible things," and then gives the striking exhortation, "Seeing ye have purified your souls in obeying the truth through the Spirit unto unfeigned love of the brethren, see that ye love one another with a pure heart fervently," and all this on the basis of the new birth which they had already received "of the incorruptible seed by the word of God."

Why, Peter, although a fisherman and an unlearned and ignorant man, yet when thou writest under the inspiration of the Holy Ghost, it is almost as hard to keep up with thee as with thy beloved brother, Paul!

See how holiness is, as it were, piled up and repeated in various ways in the sentence quoted above. (1), "Ye have purified your souls." Yes, and it was Peter who spoke before the council at Jerusalem in reference to Cornelius and his household, and said that God "put no difference between us and them, purifying their hearts by faith." The word "purify" is derived from a Greek root which means "fire." Souls are purified by the fire of the Holy Spirit, and the result is a continual "obeying the truth," and (2), the positive side of this purification is "unfeigned love of the brethren," and this is love with a pure heart and fervent, the same love which John calls perfect love, and the standard of which is in the words of the Lord Jesus, "As I have loved you that ye also love one another."

Was ever more holiness crowded into a single verse? Peter had never been to a Theological Seminary, but he had listened through three eventful years to the blessed teachings of the Lord Jesus, and he had been filled with the Holy Ghost on the day of Pentecost, and without aiming at system or explanation, he has compressed more sound theology into a single verse than we find in many a voluminous treatise and many a lengthy commentary and many an eloquent sermon.

And then in the rapturous eloquence of inspiration he tells us how to grow in grace. "Wherefore, laying aside all malice and all guile, and hypocrisies, and envies, and all evil speakings, as newborn babes desire the sincere milk of the word, that ye may grow thereby," and his last exhortation at the end of the second epistle is, "But grow in grace and in the knowledge of our Lord and Saviour, Jesus Christ."

Peter, by no means, teaches us that we grow into grace, or that we grow into entire sanctification. We first become receivers, and get grace before we can grow in it, and we must first receive entire sanctification before we can grow in it. Like all other gospel blessings, this is the gift of God, and is forever, therefore, unobtainable by any process of growth. But Peter says in effect, in order to grow in grace you must do two things. (1), Lay aside everything that hinders growth, specifying malice, guile, hypocrisies, envies, evil speakings. Now it is plain as the sun at noon-day that all these things are the fruits of the carnal mind. And so in a single thought the exhortation is to lay aside, or put off, or give up to destruction, the depravity of our nature, the inbred sin which doth so easily beset, and which so long as it exists, will be an insuperable hindrance to all rapid and symmetrical growth, and (2) desire, and of course, partake of the sincere milk of the word. Ah, here is wisdom, the secret of successful growth, in the spiritual as in the natural world, is first to become healthy, and then to take plenty of nourishment. Holiness is spiritual health, and implies the absence of inbred sin which is always spiritual disease. The child that is healthy and gets plenty of pure milk will grow and develop rapidly. The time will soon come when he can eat and digest meat and still strengthen and expand his physical organism on this richer diet, and thus he will finally become a large and strong man. But the child may be healthy and still not grow because it is starving for want of food. Or, it may have plenty of the most wholesome food and still not grow because disease prevents it from assimilating the nourishment. Sound health and plenty of food, with proper exercise, are the essentials of the right kind of growth. Now the Holy Bible contains not only milk for babes, but strong meat for strong men. It has been remarked by another that if Christians would be giants they must eat giants' food. And the essential requisite for appropriating either the milk or the meat is to have a sound spiritual constitution and that means simply entire sanctification. Peter is right again. We grow by the sincere milk of the word after we have gotten rid of that which always and everywhere obstructs true growth.

Of course my reader will not understand me to say, any more than Peter himself says, that we experience growth in grace simply by a head knowledge of the

Holy Scriptures. I do not forget that it is not the written word but the Eternal Word, the Lord Jesus Christ Himself, who is the bread of life. Nor do I forget that we feed upon His broken body and His shed blood, not by intellect, not by reason, not by culture, not by learning, but by faith.

But after all it is the Bible, or rather it is Bible truth, whether presented on the pages of inspiration or in the preached word, which is the great instrumentality employed by the Holy Spirit, in bringing men to Christ, and in feeding and nourishing and strengthening and edifying the church which has thus been gathered to Him. And so both Peter in speaking about the "sincere milk of the word," and Paul in referring to the "strong meat," by which term he characterizes the deeper spiritual truths of revelation, are leading us to Jesus, the true bread, the living bread, the bread of life.

Our apostle passes next to a most glowing description of the Christian priesthood, and again the leading idea of holiness flashes from his pen, "Ye also, as lively stones, are built up a spiritual house, an holy priest-hood, to offer up spiritual sacrifices acceptable to God by Jesus Christ." Again, "Ye are a chosen generation, a royal priesthood, an holy nation, a peculiar people." Here is our title of nobility, beloved, and who of us would exchange it for an earldom, or a dukedom or a kingdom? Not I at least.

The Jews of old received spiritual blessing very largely, and even temporal blessing also, through the mediation of an outward priesthood. And the family of priests were chosen and ordained of God Himself. "No man taketh this honor unto himself but he that is called of God, as was Aaron."

But under the Christian dispensation all God's saved people are priests as well as kings, and the sacrifices which they offer are spiritual sacrifices, the body as a living sacrifice to be consumed like a whole burnt offering in His service, "the fruit of the lips giving thanks to His name," and the doing good and communicating, that is to say, a life rich in faith and good works, such are the sacrifices with which God is well pleased. But to be a Christian priest in the sense here described must involve and does involve the idea of entire sanctification. Peter's words will not allow us to doubt that the priesthood of believers is a "holy priesthood."

Afterwards, the chief of the apostles exhorts his readers to take ill treatment patiently when they have to suffer, not for doing wrong but for doing well, and reminds us of the example of Christ, "Who did no sin, neither was guile found in His mouth; who when He was reviled, reviled not again; when He suffered, He threatened not, but committed Himself to Him that judgeth righteously; who His own self bare our sins in His own body on the tree, that we, being dead to sins, should live unto righteousness," winding up with a terse expression of the great doctrine of the atonement "by whose stripes ye were healed."

Paul would have us "dead to sin" by reckoning. Peter would have us "dead to sins" by making no response to the suggestions of Satan or the temptations which he may present to us. To be dead either to sin within us or to sins without us, implies holiness of heart, that is, entire sanctification. Praise the Lord for the perfect agreement of His two great apostles in regard to this glorious doctrine.

Still further, Peter speaks of the "holy women" of old, and exhorts Christian women to be like them, particularly in adorning themselves not with gay attire, but with inward and spiritual graces. And in his second epistle, he alludes to "holy men of God," speaking through the Old Testament as they were moved by the Holy Ghost. And here we have the best possible definition of inspiration, in regard to which volumes have been written, and very different views expressed by equally learned and candid men. But what can be more satisfactory to the humble, Christian mind than just to feel that when he reads his Bible, he is perusing the words of "holy men of God who spake as they were moved by the Holy Ghost." Such a mind will find no difficulty about inspiration.

In the last chapter of his second epistle, Peter rebukes the unbelief of the scoffers, who then believed, and whose successors still believe that the present order of the material universe will continue for an indefinite period, if not, indeed, forever. He assures us that the Lord has not forgotten, that He is not slack concerning His promises, but that the very reason why the sinful world has been spared so long is because of God's long suffering and mercy, "not willing that any should perish, but that all should come to repentance." And, then, having declared that the heavens and the earth which are now, are reserved unto fire, that the day of the Lord shall come as a thief in the night, that the elements shall melt with fervent heat, the earth also and the works that are therein shall be burned up, he exclaims with most appropriate words, "Seeing then, that all these things shall be dissolved, what manner of persons ought ye to be in all holy conversation and godliness," and this in order "that ye may be found of Him in peace, without spot and blameless."

Praise the Lord for the doctrine of entire sanctification as taught by the apostle of the circumcision. Amen.

CHAPTER IX.

ENTIRE SANCTIFICATION AS TAUGHT BY JOHN.

John, before Pentecost, was emphatically a Son of Thunder. He could forbid a man to cast out devils in the name of Jesus, because the man was not of his own particular fold. He was ready to imitate Elijah by calling down fire from heaven to destroy the Samaritans who would not extend the rites of hospitality to his Master. He was eager to have the highest possible place in the coming kingdom of his Lord, and this at whatever cost. But after Pentecost, John was *par excellence* the apostle of love. Not that his character became anything like putty. He could still rebuke evil and denounce Diotrephes, and forbid the elect lady to receive or countenance any who did not uphold the true, sound doctrines of the gospel. He was still a son of thunder against heresy and immorality, but he was preeminently, after his baptism with the Holy Ghost, a son of consolation. His soul seems absolutely absorbed in the love of God, and his exhortations to the churches, seemed all to concentrate in two special points, love God and love one another. His heart was made perfect in love on the day of Pentecost, and he never lost the blessed experience. He retained the blessing because he retained the Blesser. The Holy Comforter was his abiding guest and keeper.

The gospel of John contains many of the most profound and spiritual truths that ever fell from the lips of the Lord Jesus. And the only distinction which John accords to himself, and that always with the greatest modesty and humility, is "the disciple whom Jesus loved."

He begins his gospel with a sublime assertion of the Deity and preëxistence of Christ as the Eternal Word, then tells of the incarnation, how the Word became flesh, and we beheld His glory, how although He was the Light of the world, yet the world knew Him not, and though He came unto His own (the Jews) yet His own received Him not, but as many as did receive Him, whether Jews or Gentiles, to them gave He power to become the children of God, and this through a new birth, not of human blood, or title, or pedigree, not of man in any way whatever, but of God. It is not sufficient, therefore, to be a child of God by creation, which, indeed, all men are, but by adoption, by the reception of the Divine nature by birth. And this new birth is more fully unfolded to the Jewish Sanhedrist, Nicodemus, both as to its necessity and its nature. "Ye must be born again." "The Son of man must be lifted up." The new birth is of water and the Spirit. The water is the water of life, the gospel offered freely to all, with its cleansing and refreshing and vivifying properties so well symbolized by water, and the Holy Spirit is the effective personal agent by whom the regeneration is wrought in the heart of the penitent sinner, though His operations may be as inexplicable as the wind, which bloweth where it listeth, and is known only by its results. Then we have the hinge-text of salvation, "God so loved the world that He gave His only begotten Son, that whosoever believeth in Him should not perish but have eternal life." Thus, in this marvelous discourse with Nicodemus, we have God's love or God's grace as the source of our salvation, Christ crucified as the ground of it, and the Holy Spirit as the Divine Agent of its accomplishment. Glory be to the Triune God.

Not only the discourse of our Lord with Nicodemus on the new birth, but His discourse, also, with the woman of Samaria on true worship is given by John alone. It is remarkable that not to a Jewish Rabbi, not to the Scribes and Pharisees, not to a Jew at all, but to a heathen or semi-heathen woman, Jesus made the first recorded, positive declaration of His Messiahship, and showed her that as God is a Spirit, so they that worship Him must do so, not in any specific locality, such as Jerusalem or Mount Gerizim, and not by any prescribed form or any outward ritual, but in spirit and in truth. No wonder that her heart was immediately and completely captivated by so grand and glorious a revelation, and that, at once, she left her waterpot and went her way to become a preacher of righteousness to her fellow-townsmen.

Passing over the fifth chapter, with the appeal to the Jews to search the Scriptures and the assurance that they testified of Him; and the sixth chapter, with its story of complete self-abnegation, when after a stupendous miracle, the people were disposed to take Him by force and make Him a king, but He departed into a mountain Himself alone, and the next day, the wonderful discourse upon the bread of life, which sifted away from Him a large proportion of those who had been so ready to proclaim Him King, and brought out of the core of His heart those pathetic words to the twelve, "Will ye also go away?", we come to the seventh chapter and the feast of Tabernacles, at which, on the occasion of the priest pouring water from the pool of Siloam, out of a golden pitcher into a trumpet-shaped receptacle above the altar, amid the rejoicings of the people, Jesus stood and cried, "If any man thirst let him come unto Me and drink." "He that believeth on Me, as the Scripture hath said, from within him shall flow rivers of living water." The Scripture referred to is, probably, Isaiah 58:11, and, perhaps, other similar passages. "And the Lord shalt guide thee continually, and satisfy thy soul in drought, and make fat thy bones, and thou shalt be like a watered garden and like a spring of water, whose waters fail not."

But the beloved disciple himself gives us an extremely valuable inspired commentary on these words of the Lord Jesus, in order that readers in all ages might make the true spiritual application which is intended by them. "But this spake He of the Spirit which they that believe on Him should receive, for the Holy Ghost was not yet given, because that Jesus was not yet glorified." These remarkable words seem to clearly imply that notwithstanding the presence and operation of the Spirit in the former dispensations of God's grace, yet He was to be poured out on all God's children under the gospel in a sense and to an extent, which so far transcends the highest manifestation of His power in Old Testament times that in comparison it is said the Holy Ghost was not yet given, or, literally, the Holy Ghost was not yet. And this wondrous outpouring was to be after the glorification of Jesus and as a consequence of that glorification. So that Pentecost, with its untold wealth of privilege, could not be realized till after the death, resurrection and ascension of the Lord Jesus Christ.

And we are clearly informed that what the church of the hundred and twenty received on the day of

Pentecost, namely, the purifying of their hearts by faith and the enduement of power, that is to say, entire sanctification, with all its blessed accompaniments, was not a privilege confined to apostolic times, and to the opening of the Holy Ghost dispensation; for Peter boldly assured the wondering multitude that the promise of the same blessed experience "is to you and to your children and to all that are afar off, even as many as the Lord our God shall call." And thus it is for the church and for every individual believer, until Christ Himself shall come again. God help all Christians everywhere to see and to believe and to realize it. Amen.

In the eighth chapter, we are told how Jesus showed the slavery of sin. "Every one that committeth sin is the bond-servant of sin," and coupled with this the glorious announcement that, "If the Son, therefore, shall make you free, ye shall be free indeed." Yes, Jesus came to free us not simply from the guilt and the condemnation and the penalty of sin, but from that which brings guilt and condemnation and penalty, even from sin itself.

Here is true Christian liberty, and it does not mean license, it does not mean do as you please, it does not mean the liberty of making your own choices, but it does mean be pleased with what pleases God, and in this manner after all you will do as you please, it means the glad acceptance of God's choices. And so, after all, you do have your own way because it is God's way, it means liberty and choice to do everything right and nothing wrong, or to do right in all directions and wrong in none. May God bring all His children out of slavery and into freedom for Jesus' sake.

In the memorable discourse of the Lord Jesus with His disciples at the last supper, as given by John in the 14th, 15th and 16th chapters of his gospel, He told them of the blessed Comforter, "which is the Holy Ghost," whom the Father would send in His name, and as to the method of His coming He says, "If a man love Me, he will keep My words; and My Father will love him, and We will come unto him and make Our abode with him." Here, I think, beyond a doubt, that the "We" refers to the Father and the Son, and the manner of Their coming and indwelling in the heart of the believer is through Their representative, the Holy Spirit. And if this be true, how is it possible that such a heart in which Father, Son and Holy Ghost abide, should not be sanctified wholly?

In his first Epistle, the beloved apostle develops beautifully the doctrine of perfect love. He declares that God's children must not walk in darkness or sin, and that those who do so cannot, truthfully, claim to have fellowship with Him. "But if we walk in the light, as He is in the light, we have fellowship one with another," (which implies fellowship with God) "and the blood of Jesus Christ, His Son, cleanseth from all sin."

This is a very striking and all-important statement. The verb is in the present tense, and denotes a present and a continuous action. It cleanseth persistently and continuously. You trust in Jesus this moment, and the blood cleanseth now, another moment and it cleanseth, and thus on, without intermission or cessation. And the cleansing is from all sin, sin committed and sin inbred, sin in act, word or thought, sin outward and sin inward, sin open and sin secret, sin of knowledge and sin of ignorance, literally and truly all sin. If this does not mean entire sanctification, what use is there in language as an expression of thought? Surely none.

But the objection is strongly urged by some that the next verse assures us that "If we say that we have no sin we deceive ourselves and the truth is not in us." But why sunder this verse from its appropriate connections? Were there not Pharisees in the time of Christ who would not admit that they were sinners, and would not accept the baptism of repentance from John the Baptist? And did not the Apostle John live to see the germs of incipient gnosticism showing themselves in the church, assuming, like modern Christian science, that all evil is in matter, the soul is immaculate, and some Gnostics even believing that it was possible to have fellowship with God while living in all kinds of sensual indulgence and licentiousness, and moreover denying the reality of the incarnation of Christ, as also of the crucifixion and resurrection? These were the Docetists or Phantasiasts, so well described by Longfellow:

"Ah, to how many faith has been
No evidence of things unseen,
But a dim shadow, which recasts
The creed of the Phantasiasts,
For whom no man of sorrows died:
For whom the tragedy divine
Was but a symbol and a sign,
And Christ a phantom crucified."

Now John in the passage referred to, tells us that on certain conditions it is possible to experience through the blood of Christ, which means simply the merits of His atoning and vicarious sacrifice, a complete cleansing from all sin, and then turning to those who deny that they are sinners, he exclaims, and if we say that we have no sin, and therefore do not need this cleansing, and can do without this atonement, then we deceive ourselves and the truth is not in us. How much more rational is such an interpretation than the exposition which makes one verse contradict the other, and represents the apostle as first assuring us that we may be cleansed from all sin, and then declaring in effect. "But be sure to remember that this cleansing is never really affected, and you are never really without sin."

There are so many rich and blessed teachings in this epistle that we must needs make selection and leave many passages to be carefully and prayerfully pondered by the reader, with the assurance that there is very much gold to be found for the digging; but we would call attention in a special manner to John's description of perfect love. "There is no fear in love; but perfect love casteth out fear, because fear hath torment. He that feareth is not made perfect in love."

It is clearly to be inferred from these expressions that whilst all Christians do and must love God, yet there is a stage denominated perfect love, which many Christians have not yet reached. And this stage of religious experience is marked distinctly by the absence of fear. Most certainly our apostle does not mean for us to understand that we shall ever get beyond that reverential and filial fear, which is the right and proper accompaniment of our childlike relation to our Heavenly Father. But he specially describes the fear that will be gotten rid of as tormenting fear, and this fear he declares that "perfect love casteth out." Now we can readily see the reasonableness of this statement. Fear about the future, whether as to temporal or spiritual things, fear of evil tidings, fear of man, fear of death, in short, all tormenting fear is caused by the presence of inbred sin. As a matter of course, therefore, when sin is cast out, fear is cast out with it. Now perfect love is the positive side of entire sanctification; it implies the absence of inbred sin and the unmixed love of God occupying the soul. Such love, therefore, most truly must cast out fear.

The impenitent sinner neither fears nor loves God. The awakened sinner fears him, but does not love Him. The justified believer both fears and loves. Sometimes the fear is in the ascendant and sometimes the love. The entirely sanctified believer loves with all his heart, and has no tormenting fear. Praise the Lord.

And the beloved apostle instructs us also as to the method of obtaining the blessing of perfect love. It is by the prayer of faith, and the prayer of faith involves the idea of a preceding entire consecration. "For," says John, "if our heart condemn us, God is greater than our heart," which probably signifies that He also will condemn us, and, therefore, we cannot utter a believing prayer for such a blessing as entire sanctification while we are not wholly given up to the Lord, for while that is our case, our heart will continue to condemn us.

But he continues, "If our heart condemn us not, then have we confidence towards God." And again, "This is the confidence that we have in Him, that if we ask anything according to His will, He heareth us; and if we know that He hear us, whatsoever we ask we know that we have the petitions that we desired of Him."

Nowhere is the philosophy of the plan of full salvation

more beautifully portrayed than in these precious words. We are shown here that (1), the seeker of entire sanctification must be wholly consecrated to God. (2), That he must pray in faith. (3), That he must pray according to God's will. (4), That then he may know that he has the very thing he asks for. Here is wisdom. Let every seeker act upon it. Amen.

Nor does John leave us in doubt as to the witness of the Spirit to our conscious cleansing. "If we love one another" (i.e. with a true and pure and unselfish and self-sacrificing Christian love) "God dwelleth in us and His love is perfected in us." "Hereby know we that we dwell in Him and He in us, because He hath given us of His Spirit." Now to have God's love perfected in us, and to have Him to dwell in us, can mean nothing less than entire sanctification, and we know this, as John tells us, by His Spirit. We have, therefore, the witness of the Spirit to perfect love as well as to adoption.

CHAPTER X.

ENTIRE SANCTIFICATION AS TAUGHT BY JAMES AND JUDE.

James and Jude were brothers. They were also "brethren of the Lord." Whether this expression means actual brothers, namely, children of Joseph and Mary, or whether it means only cousins, also whether these two men were apostles or not, are questions which I leave to the Biblical critics. Receiving without argument their respective epistles as belonging to the inspired canon, I am to inquire what their teaching is in reference to the one theme of this book, that is, entire sanctification.

James, as a writer, is intensely practical. As Bishop of Jerusalem he presided specially over the Jewish Christian Church, and his epistle is addressed "to the twelve tribes which are scattered abroad," i.e., to the Jews of the Dispersion, primarily, no doubt, to the Christian Jews, but also secondarily and by way of warning to the unconverted Jews. James was "zealous of the law." He fully agreed with Paul and with Peter that the yoke of circumcision and the Mosaic law was not to be imposed upon the Gentile Churches, but he, no doubt, strongly insisted that Jewish converts should be still very careful to observe the outward law. His epistle is like Matthew's gospel, and savors strongly of the Sermon on the Mount. As a bishop and overseer of a Jewish flock of Christians, while he fully assented to Paul's teaching on justification by faith, he, nevertheless, urged upon the people with vehemence that they should show their faith by their works and that they should be "doers of the word and not hearers only." As Paul completely demolishes the doctrine of salvation by the works of the law, so James in his epistle offers us an inspired and a vigorous protest against every form of Antinomianism. Thus the two writers, both moved by the Holy Ghost, present the two aspects of gospel truth so plainly that he may run that readeth. "We are saved by faith, not by works," says Paul. "Aye," says James, "but we are saved in good works, not out of them," and we must be careful to maintain good works, not in order to be saved, but because we are saved. Good works are necessary, not as the ground or the cause of salvation, but as the fruit and resultant and test of the salvation which we have received by faith. James, therefore, is not antagonistic to, but only complementary of the great apostle of the Gentiles.

And mark how he strikes or aims right at the mark of Christian perfection in the very beginning of his epistle. He assures us that if we let patience have her perfect work, we shall be perfect and entire, wanting nothing.

Christian perfection, then, according to James. is perfect patience. Christian perfection according to John, is perfect love. Christian perfection, according to Paul, is maturity or being "thoroughly furnished unto all good works." Christian perfection, according to Peter, is in being established, strengthened, settled. Surely none but a caviller will find any want of harmony between these different modes of expression. They all imply deliverance from sin, which is always instantaneous, and some of them imply a mature Christian character, which is always gradual.

James gives a vivid description of inbred sin under the name of lust. "Every man is tempted when he is drawn away of his own lust and enticed. Then when lust hath conceived it bringeth forth (actual) sin; and sin when it is finished bringeth forth death."

We cannot doubt that James, like the other writers of the Bible, believed in a personal devil, for he speaks of a wisdom which is "devilish" and if a man is enticed to sin by the natural depravity of his heart, we must not overlook the fact that the enticement implies an enticer, and that the wicked spiritual adversary of our race knows how to adapt his baits to the peculiar form in which inbred sin is strongest in each individual, and thus, if possible, to entrap and destroy him. Depravity exists by nature in all, but in one man it is particularly felt in the direction of covetousness, in another, of pride, in another, of ambition, in another, of sensuality. Satan's temptations in the first of these would most likely be something which holds out the prospect of getting gain by sinning; in the second, it would be something to feed his intense admiration of self, to cherish his pride; in the third, it would be the hope of political or some other kind of power on the condition of sacrificing principle; in the fourth, it would be the gratification of bodily appetites as in drunkenness, gluttony, or licentiousness. Thus the trap is set for every man, and the trapper is wary. God save us from his wiles.

And as Peter tells us to lay aside inbred sin, as it exists

in the form of malice, and guile, and hypocrisies, and envies, and shows itself in evil speakings, so James tells us to lay apart "all filthiness and superfluity of naughtiness," or "overflowing of wickedness." Ah, beloved, most truly did Jesus say that the heart of man is a fountain of wickedness, out of the heart of man proceed evil thoughts and all actual sins; yes, there is by nature in each one of us a superfluity of naughtiness, an overflowing of wickedness, a natural depravity, an inbred sin, and this must be "laid apart," it must be gotten rid of by bringing and subjecting the heart where it dwells to the fiery baptism with the Holy Ghost, and then shall we be in a position to receive, with meekness, the engrafted word, which is able to save our souls.

St. James speaks of the "law of liberty," and of the "royal law," the latter being, "Thou shalt love thy neighbor as thyself," and both mean, I apprehend, just what we have already alluded to as the law of love. "Love," says Paul, "is the fulfilling of the law," and this is liberty, and this is royalty, the freedom to do God's will because we love it, and to have all the antagonisms to that blessed will expelled from our hearts, and all lawful affections and passions subdued and subjected to Him who is our King, and who reigns without a rival in our hearts.

"I worship Thee, sweet will of God,
  And all Thy ways adore;
And every day I live, I seem
  To love Thee more and more."

If this is not the true liberty and the true royalty, where shall we find them? Not on earth, at least.

James does not spend words in exhorting us to seek more religion, but he tersely defines pure religion. And that is what we want. It does not depend upon age, nor size, nor growth. A stalk of corn may be pure as soon as it raises itself above the surface of the ground. Another stalk may be impure and diseased when it is many feet in height. A Christian may seek and find pure religion and undefiled, very soon after he is born again. Another Christian may spend years and years in seeking more religion, and yet not become the possessor of purity of heart.

This pure religion, according to our author, consists in works of beneficence and love as to its outward manifestations, but its true inward principle is in keeping one's self "unspotted from the world." Oh, that all my readers with myself, may thus keep themselves unspotted from the world, which involves the idea of being sanctified wholly, and in the end "may be found of Him in peace without spot and blameless."

But an objector here interposes with a quotation from James which is supposed to preclude the possibility of living without sin. "In many things we offend all." But this expression is not to be thus interpreted. To make it mean that all Christians must continue in the commission of sin to the end of their lives, would not only be doing violence to that which is the very trend of our author's teaching, namely, a spotless morality and a pure and holy life, but it would also prove too much. For a little further on we read, in reference to that unruly evil, the tongue, "Therewith bless we God, even the Father; and therewith curse we men which are made after the similitude of God," and again, "Behold, we put bits in the horses' mouths that they may obey us, and we turn about their whole body." Surely no expositor would maintain from such language that James was a tamer of horses and a profane swearer. The truth is, that James, out of kindness and courtesy, includes himself among his hearers or readers, and means to show us how liable we are to give offence through rash and ill-advised words, and then, on the other hand, he does not fail to mention the man who does not offend in word, and who is able, by the grace of God, to bridle the whole body, that is, to live without sin, and whom, again, he styles a "perfect man."

Our author further informs us that heavenly, divine wisdom is first pure, then peaceable. The carnal Christian, or babe in Christ, would often reverse this arrangement. He is clamorous for peace, often to the extent that he would have a wisdom that is first peaceable and then pure, but the Holy Ghost puts purity first, and He is always right. No compromise must be made with error in doctrine, or evil in practice, even for the sake of peace. But when we become possessors of a wisdom which is first pure, then, also, the other qualities follow in proper succession, peaceable, gentle, easy to be entreated and the rest.

Listen, again, to the stern moralist and preacher of holiness, "Cleanse your hands, ye sinners, and purify your hearts, ye double minded." Here, again, we can but thankfully admire the perfect accuracy of the Holy Ghost, as regards the method of full salvation. To cleanse the hands is to obtain pardon and absolution for what we have done, and it is always the first work of the unsaved man to repent and seek the forgiveness of his sins. When this forgiveness has been obtained, then his hands are cleansed, but he may still be double-minded. He may still be unstable in all his ways. His spiritual course may still be zig-zag. His life may still be a series of sinning and repenting, and sinning again and repenting again, till he cries out in his misery, "O wretched man that I am, who (not what) shall deliver me from this body of death?" And then James's prescription comes home to him, "Purify your hearts, ye double-minded." Seek and obtain the blessing of entire sanctification, and, henceforth, with one mind and one purpose, run joyfully in the way of Christ's commandments. Justification first and entire sanctification afterwards. First cleanse your hands, then purify your hearts. And with this agree the words of the Psalmist, "Who shall ascend into the hill of the Lord? or who shall stand in His holy place?" "He that hath clean hands," that is, whose sins have been pardoned, "and a pure heart," that is, who has been sanctified wholly. The teachings of the Holy Ghost are marvelously harmonious in the Old Testament and the New.

Finally, James assures us that the "prayer of faith shall save the sick, and the Lord shall raise him up." And not only physical but spiritual blessing may be received in the same way for "If he have committed sins, they shall be forgiven him." His conclusion is that "The supplication of a righteous man availeth much in its working," R.V., but I prefer to regard the Greek participle in the original as in the passive voice, and then the meaning would be, as suggested by Dr. S.A. Keen in his Faith papers, "The prayer of a righteous man being energized" (by the Holy Ghost) "availeth much."

I should understand the "prayer of faith," therefore, to be a prayer begotten in the heart of the believer by the Holy Ghost, and with the prayer is communicated also the corresponding faith, and when this is the case, the answer is sure. Faith, in this use of the word, is a special gift, and may be given to some and withheld from others, also given at one time and withheld at another, just as God in His infinite and unerring wisdom may decide. This kind of faith is one of the special gifts of which we have an account in the 12th of 1st Corinthians, and differs, therefore, from the grace of faith or the power of believing the gospel unto salvation when it is presented, which is given to all men, and for the exercise of which, by actually believing, all are held responsible. "He that believeth shall be saved, and he that believeth not shall be condemned."

And it is Jude, the brother of James, who exhorts his readers to pray in the Holy Ghost, the very same kind of praying which James calls the prayer of faith, and about which Paul also declares that "the Spirit Himself also helpeth our infirmities, for we know not what we should pray for as we ought; but the Spirit Himself maketh intercession for with groanings which cannot be uttered. And He that searcheth the hearts knoweth what is the mind of the Spirit, because He maketh intercession for the saints according to the will of God."

A Holy Ghost prayer, therefore, such as Jude alludes to, is a prayer that is energized by the Holy Ghost. It is not the Holy Ghost who does the groaning, but He causes the heart of the consecrated believer to groan, by kindling those intense desires after some specific blessing, which often are, indeed, too deep for clear expression by utterance, and with the groanings, also, the faith is given, which takes hold of God's Almightiness for the answer. Such prayers do, indeed, move the hand that moves the world, and whether it be for the healing of the sick, or the conversion of sinners, or the entire sanctification of believers, or the supply of temporal needs, or anything else which the Holy Spirit may suggest, the blessing is sure to come.

I am not forgetting that the assistance of the Holy Spirit is needed, and that it is obtainable in all true prayer, but ordinary prayer must be founded upon the promises of God and an exercise of will power to believe those promises, and therefore, it must be accompanied, in order to be effectual, by ordinary faith, the act of believing. Extraordinary prayer must be inspired directly by the Holy Spirit, and the gift of faith must come directly from Him. So that we have ordinary prayer, ordinary faith and ordinary results in the one case, while in the other, we have extraordinary prayer, extraordinary faith and extraordinary results. Praise the Lord.

Jude tells us that as Christian believers we are to "hate even the garment spotted by the flesh," that is, to keep entirely clear of all the pollutions of sin, symbolized by the garment of the leper which was regarded as unclean, and which passage, when spiritually interpreted, must mean the unspotted holiness of the true Christian. And as to the question of one's ability to live without sin, he commits us to the care of Him who is "able to keep us from falling," the very thing we need and which we cannot do for ourselves, and "to present us faultless before the presence of His glory with exceeding joy." First, then, we are to be sanctified wholly, then kept from falling by the power of Christ through the indwelling Spirit. Finally, presented without spot, blameless and faultless in the presence of

God's glory in heaven. And this is the gospel according to Jude.

Dougan Clark

CHAPTER XI.

SANCTIFIED BY GOD THE FATHER.

There is one expression in the epistle of Jude, which I purposely omitted in the preceding chapter, that it might have a more prominent place in the present one.

Nowhere else in the Bible are we expressly declared to be "sanctified by God the Father." It is cause of rejoicing, however, that every person of the Godhead, every member of the adorable Trinity, is concerned in the sanctification of a human soul. And this fact, like many others, points to the extreme importance of the subject on which we are treating; for if the working of God the Father, God the Son and God the Holy Spirit is required, and is brought into active operation in order to cleanse our hearts from the pollution of sin, and fit us for heaven, then it must be in the estimation of the triune God, a matter of prime necessity that we should be thus cleansed. If God, therefore, regards it as an essential that we be sanctified wholly, let us beware of the thought that it is only optional, that it is possible, if possible at all, only for the few and not for the many, and that it can be done without, or what is practically too nearly the same thing, postponed until we see, or think we see, the near approach of death. What every person of the Godhead is urging upon our acceptance now, let us not dare either to reject or postpone.

"Behold, now is the accepted time; behold, now is the day of salvation."

Paul said to the Ephesian elders at Miletus, "And now, brethren, I commend you to God, and to the word of His grace, which is able to build you up and to give you an inheritance among all them which are sanctified."

Ah, beloved reader, we can never estimate the debt we owe to the unbounded grace of God. Grace means unmerited favor. Grace is God's infinite love in active working for the salvation of man. And, the source of our sanctification, just as of our justification, and indeed of every gospel blessing provided for us, is the grace of God. And when our souls are stirred up to ecstatic gratitude and love, by the thought of the "unspeakable gift" of the Lord Jesus Christ, and of the unspeakable blessings derived from and through Him, let us not forget that behind it all and over it all, is the broad and incomprehensible declaration, "God so loved the world, that He gave His only begotten Son."

Absolute sovereignty, authority, supremacy and paternity belong to God the Father. The Father sends the Son. The Father and the Son send the Holy Spirit. Neither the Son nor the Spirit, nor both together, ever send the Father. The Father "created all things by Jesus Christ." Jesus Christ cast out devils "by the Spirit of God." The Son reveals the Father, for "no man knoweth the Father save the Son, and he to whomso-ever the Son will reveal Him." And the Holy Spirit reveals Jesus, for "no man can say that Jesus is Lord but by the Holy Ghost." "He shall testify of Me." "He shall take of Mine and show it unto you." "He shall not speak of Himself; but what He shall hear" (from the

Father and the Son) "that shall He speak."

Thus the greatest gift that God the Father has given or could give to His creature man is the gift of His Son. The greatest gift that God the Son has given to man after He gave Himself for us is the gift of the Holy Ghost, for it is not only said, "I will pray the Father and He shall give you another Comforter," and "whom the Father will send in My name," but also, "If I depart I will send Him unto you," so we may say in general terms, that the Holy Ghost as a personal sanctifier, energizer and Comforter, is the promise of the Father and the gift of the Son. And it may be added that the greatest gift of the Holy Spirit to man is the gift of entire sanctification or perfect love. Glory be to God the Father, God the Son and God the Holy Ghost. Amen.

And thus when Jude tells us that we are sanctified by God the Father, He means not only that we are separated unto the gospel of life and salvation, set apart to God and His service, but, also, that God the Father has made ample provision in the death of His Son for all Christian believers to be cleansed from every stain of moral defilement, delivered from inbred sin, sanctified wholly, made perfect in love, and filled with the Spirit. We repeat, therefore, that it will be a matter of eternal thankfulness and gratitude to the redeemed soul, that the source of all these unspeakable blessings is in the infinite grace and love of God.

Everywhere throughout the Old Testament, the holiness of God is brought prominently forward and insisted upon. And His own holiness is presented as a sufficient reason why His people should be holy also. "Be ye holy, for I am holy," which command and declaration are repeated and endorsed by the Apostle Peter in his first epistle, "But as He which hath called you is holy, so be ye holy in all manner of conversation, because it is written, Be ye holy, for I am holy."

As God the Father, therefore, is Himself infinitely holy, and He requires all His children to be holy even in the present life, it goes without saying, as already shown, that He makes provision in His gospel for them to be made and kept holy. And it is precisely the standard of God's holiness which is set before us by the Saviour as the mark at which we also are to aim, and aim not vainly nor unsuccessfully. "Be ye perfect even as your Father in heaven is perfect." Not that our perfection or our holiness can be equal to His in degree. That would make the finite equal to the infinite, and would be an impossibility and absurdity, but that we are to be perfect in our sphere as He is perfect in His, that we are to be holy with the same kind of holiness that appertains to Him, in a word, that we are to be perfect in love as He is perfect love, and that we are to be delivered from all sin, not by any effort or any merit of our own but by His unmerited grace in Christ Jesus. Let us rejoice and praise His name that we are sanctified by God the Father.

CHAPTER XII.

SANCTIFIED BY GOD THE SON.

As the source of our entire sanctification is in the unmerited love and grace of God the Father, so the ground of it is in the blood of Christ the Son. Justification and Sanctification are by no means identical, but as regards the origin, the ground, and the means, they are precisely parallel. We are told that justification is by grace, and, again, that it is by the blood of Jesus, and, still again, that it is by faith. It is, therefore, God's grace, it is Christ's blood, it is man's faith by which we are justified. The originating cause of our justification is the grace of God. The procuring cause is the blood of Jesus Christ. The instrumental cause is our own faith.

And all this is equally true of our entire sanctification. We are not justified in one way and sanctified in another. We are sanctified as well as justified by the grace of God. We are sanctified as well as justified by the blood of Christ. We are sanctified as well as justified by our own faith.

All gospel blessings are founded upon the vicarious sacrifice of the Lord Jesus Christ. He "of God is made unto us wisdom and righteousness, (justification) and sanctification and redemption."

And sanctification, no more than justification, releases us from our dependence upon the atonement. If we are either justified or sanctified today it is not because we deserve it, but because Christ died for us. If we shall be either justified or sanctified at any future period of our eternity, it will not be because we deserve it but because Christ died for us. And so forever and forever we shall need the merit of His death, and we shall rejoice to join in the song of redemption "unto Him that loved us, and washed us from our sins in His own blood, and hath made us kings and priests unto God and His Father; to Him be glory and dominion forever and ever. Amen." We are everlastingly linked to the atonement of Jesus Christ, and this both for the pardon of past sins, and the entire cleansing of the heart.

"Thou shalt call His name Jesus because He shall save His people from their sins," which signifies, I apprehend, both the forgiveness of sins already committed and saving them from the commission of sins in the future. Here, then, we have justification and regeneration. "Behold the Lamb of God who taketh away the sin of the world." This must mean the sin of our nature, the sin that dwelleth in us, the sin that doth so easily beset us, in a word, inbred sin. And to have the inbred sin taken away means nothing more and nothing less and nothing else, than entire sanctification. Yes, beloved, we are sanctified by God the Son.

"The blood of Jesus Christ, His Son, cleanseth us from all sin." Here we have a positive statement that upon certain conditions to be fulfilled by us, we shall experience a cleansing from outward sin, and inward sin, and sin of ignorance, and conscious sin, and open sin and secret sin, and all sin. There is no mistaking the length and breadth and all comprehensiveness of this glorious promise. Beloved, let us walk in the light as He is in the light, and so know, for ourselves, that this wondrous declaration is divinely true.

And this is a result of His atoning sacrifice, which result He had in view, no less than the removal of our guilt when He laid down His life for us. "Wherefore, Jesus, also, that He might sanctify the people with His own blood, suffered without the gate." Glory to His Name.

He died, therefore, not alone that we might be saved from guilt and condemnation and penalty, but that we might be saved from sin, or sanctified wholly. And I would that every one of my Christian readers might unite in the hymn.

"The cleansing stream I see, I see,
I plunge and oh, it cleanseth me.
It cleanseth me. Yes, cleanseth me."

CHAPTER XIII.

SANCTIFIED BY GOD THE HOLY GHOST.

As already intimated all the persons of the adorable Trinity are concerned in the work of entirely sanctifying a human soul. And this is naturally to be expected, because God is one Trinitarianism is not Tritheism. In essence one, in personality three, such is the revelation of Holy Scripture in regard to the eternal Godhead. The Bible reveals the fact, but does not reveal the how. We bow in adoring gratitude and love before an incomprehensible mystery, and rejoice in believing even without understanding.

Now the Holy Spirit is regarded by nearly all Christians as distinctively and specially the Sanctifier, "The renewing of the Holy Ghost which He shed on us abundantly through Jesus Christ, our Saviour," is spoken of in the epistle to Titus in direct connection with the "washing of regeneration," and seems intended to be experienced just after it. Possibly the renewing here spoken of, may signify only the change of heart wrought by the Holy Ghost at the new birth, but possibly, also, the apostle had in mind the entire cleansing of the heart from sin. And in that case the renewing need not be any more gradual or progressive than the washing, which all admit to be instantaneous.

Peter, in describing, to the Church at Jerusalem, the occurrences which he had witnessed at the house of Cornelius in Cesarea, used this language: "And God which knoweth the hearts, bare them witness, giving them the Holy Ghost, even as He did unto us, and put no difference between us and them, purifying their hearts by faith." Evidently here the chief of the apostles gives us to understand that the giving of the Holy Ghost, and the purifying of the heart by faith, are co-instantaneous and identical experiences. And if this be so, the Holy Ghost, who is a Divine person, and not a mere influence, must be the effective agent in purifying the heart, that is to say, it is He who by His Divine energy sanctifies us wholly.

And with this agree the words of John the Baptist: "I indeed baptize you with water, unto repentance, but He that cometh after me is mightier than I, whose shoes I am not worthy to bear. He shall baptize you with the Holy Ghost and with fire." For what purpose is this fiery baptism with the Holy Ghost? Most certainly that it may consume the inbred sin of our nature, as fire consumes the chaff, or destroys the alloy that the gold may be left pure.

Paul in his epistle to the Romans uses the following language, viz: "That I should be the minister of Jesus Christ to the Gentiles, ministering the gospel of God that the offering up of the Gentiles might be acceptable, being sanctified by the Holy Ghost." This great apostle was the first to clearly understand the perfect equality between Jew and Gentile in the gospel of salvation, and as he made hundreds of Gentile converts in His extensive missionary journeys, and offered them up with their own consent and co-operation in entire consecration to God, they were sanctified by the Holy Ghost.

The same apostle says to the Thessalonians, "We are bound to give thanks always to God for you, brethren, beloved of the Lord, because God hath from the beginning chosen you to salvation through sanctification of the Spirit and belief of the truth." This is the true election and the true salvation, a salvation from sin, through sanctification of the Spirit and this is to be obtained by faith.

And the apostle of the circumcision uses language very similar in addressing the Jewish Christians who are scattered abroad, and whom he addresses as "Elect according to the foreknowledge of God the Father, through sanctification of the Spirit, unto obedience and sprinkling of the blood of Jesus Christ." Comparing these two citations we observe again, that the blood of Jesus Christ is the ground of our sanctification, and by a continuous sprinkling we may have a continuous cleansing, and also that the Holy Spirit is the effective agent in applying that precious blood, and in sanctifying our souls, on condition that we believe the truth. God help all Christians to be not faithless, but believing.

CHAPTER XIV.

SANCTIFIED BY THE TRUTH.

We have just seen that the Spirit operates in the work of sanctification in connection with belief of the truth on our part. And with this agree the words of our Lord in His intercessory prayer. "Sanctify them through Thy truth. Thy word is truth." The word here is not the eternal Logos, but God's revealed truth as given in Holy writ. And it is a statement of the highest importance, made by Him who is the truth, that the medium or means of our sanctification is in the truth of God as made known to us in the gospel of His Son. Here, again, the Apostle Peter gives expression to the same sentiment when he says: "Whereby are given unto us exceeding great and precious promises; that by these ye might be partakers of the Divine nature having escaped the corruption that is in the world through lust." If we are favored to escape the corruption that is in the world, we are sanctified wholly, and this is effected, Peter says, not by works of righteousness, not by resolutions or penances, not by striving to do holiness, before we seek to be holy, but by faith in the promises of God. These promises are very numerous, and varied in character on the pages of the Bible. By seizing upon them as written specially for us, we make them our own, and they become in and by Jesus Christ yea and amen, that is to say, we realize them in our own experience to be the truth, and thus when we read "This is the will of God even your sanctification," or, "The very God of peace sanctify you wholly," or, "I will circumcise your heart," or "I will put my Spirit within you and cause you to walk in my statutes," immediately the truth is impressed upon our hearts as a glorious reality, and we are enabled to reckon ourselves dead, indeed, unto sin, and alive unto God, and to realize that the Saviour's prayer is answered and we are in His own blessed words, sanctified "by the truth." If any reader will take a concordance and look for the word truth, and search out the passages containing it, he will be convinced that, however men may look at it, we have to do with the Lord God of truth, and that His estimate of truth is so high that He will by no means countenance any person or anything that liveth or maketh a lie. And if we would honor Him, we must honor His truth, the truth that is to make us free from the bondage of inbred sin, the truth which we are commanded to buy, whatever may be the price, and sell it not, the truth which the Lord desires in the inward parts as well as upon the lips, the truth of God, the truth of holiness, the truth by which we are sanctified, the truth of the word.

And then we shall find in our own experience that "A God of truth and without iniquity, just and right is He," that He will send out His light and His truth that they may bring us to His holy hill and to His tabernacle, that He has given us a banner, even the banner of holiness to the Lord, to be displayed because of the truth, and we must never let it trail in the dust, that His truth shall be our shield and buckler, and that while the law was given by Moses, grace and truth came by Jesus Christ.

Glory be to His precious name forever, who is the truth.

CHAPTER XV.

SANCTIFIED BY FAITH.

The faith-faculty was given to man at His first creation. Adam believed God and was obedient and happy, and the first thing that the wily tempter attacked, and, alas, with too much success, was man's faith. "Yea," hath God said, and "Ye shall not surely die." First, a question. Then, a doubt of God's truth; then, a doubt of His love, and the rest was easy. Man stood so long as he did stand by faith. He fell when he did fall by unbelief.

God could not be God if He did not have faith in Himself. Man could not be the child of God if he did not have faith in God. Faith binds us in the closest spiritual union with our Father in heaven. Unbelief severs this bond of union and separates us from our Creator and Redeemer. Beloved, let us have faith in God.

"Ye are all the children of God by faith in Jesus Christ." This is the Christian's pedigree. It is true that in a broad and subordinate sense all men are the children of God since He created them all. And this was known even to a Greek poet, as quoted by Paul at Athens, "For we are also His offspring." But we must not fail to remember that in John's gospel we have this statement, viz: "As many as received Him, to them gave He power to become the sons of God, even to them that believe on His name." So that it is through faith that we become the children of God, not only by creation, not only by adoption, but by birth, "Ye must be born again." "Believe on the Lord Jesus Christ and thou shalt be saved." "He that believeth on the Son hath everlasting life: and he that believeth not the Son shall not see life, but the wrath of God abideth on him." Now, the faith-faculty, or the grace of faith, or the power of believing God's truth, when it is presented, is given to all mankind. But the exercise of that power which is actual and saving faith, often requires the coöperation of the human will. And, therefore, God commands us to believe, and holds us responsible for obedience to that command. "He that believeth and is baptized shall be saved; but he that disbelieveth shall be condemned." R.V.

Thus, it is that we are saved by faith. And this is true not only in religion, but in science as well, and not in science only, but in daily life and daily business as well. Many of the well-established truths of science are matters of faith, and not of demonstration. All intelligent people believe that there is a hidden force which they call the attraction of gravitation. Nobody can tell what it is, nobody can prove its existence. It is received and adopted by faith, and serves as an excellent working hypothesis. That is all. Those who accept the undulatory theory of light are necessitated to believe that all space is pervaded by an exceedingly tenuous fluid which is called ether, and that it is in this medium that the waves of light from self-luminous bodies are produced. Nobody has demonstrated the existence of this ether. It is, for the present, accepted by faith, and explains the phenomena of light better than any other hypothesis propounded. Science is saved by faith. The home is saved by faith. If want of confidence comes between the husband and wife, or between parents and children, farewell to all the enjoyment of home life.

Finance, commerce, trade are all saved by faith. When business men, manufacturers or merchants lose faith in one another, or in their government, investments cease, machinery stops, panics occur, and hard times are complained of. As faith is the bond that binds men to God, so it is the bond that binds men one to another. When confidence is lost, all is lost. Even a solvent bank may be broken, from a sudden run upon it, caused by want of faith. Now, as faith is the substance of things hoped for, because it makes them real, as it is the evidence of things not seen, because it convinces the mind of the actual existence of the invisible, let us apply this thought to the matter in hand that, namely, of entire sanctification.

Paul in his valedictory to the Ephesian elders said to them, "And now, brethren, I commend you to God and to the word of His grace, which is able to build you up and give you an inheritance among all them which are sanctified," and in the commission to Paul himself the Saviour says, "To open their eyes, and to turn them from darkness to light, and from the power of Satan unto God, that they may receive forgiveness of sins, and inheritance among them which are sanctified by faith that is in me." And as mentioned elsewhere, sanctification of the Spirit is used by the apostle in direct connection with belief of the truth. There can be no doubt, therefore, that the instrumental means of entire sanctification is faith in the Lord Jesus Christ. "This is the confidence," says the beloved John, "that we have in Him, that if we ask anything according to His will, He heareth us, and if we know that He hear us whatsoever we ask, we know that we have the petitions that we desired of Him."

Let the consecrated believer, then, ask for a clean heart, ask for perfect love, ask for entire sanctification, ask for the baptism with the Holy Ghost, and he knows he is asking according to the will of God. Then, according to John, he knows that he is heard, and knows also by faith, because it is God's promise that he has the petitions he desired of Him. That is to say, when he thus prays, he is to put forth the act of faith, by an actual volition and will to believe that he has the clean heart, the perfect love, the entire sanctification, the Holy Ghost baptism, which he asked for. And this will be honoring God by taking Him at His word. It will be the first evidence that he is sanctified wholly, the evidence of faith, and the other evidence, the witness of the Spirit may be prayed for and waited for, but, in the meantime, he can and must rely with unwavering confidence upon the evidence or witness of faith alone. God never sends the witness of the Spirit till we honor Him by accepting the witness of faith.

I said we must believe by an act of the will. And some reader may object to this statement by asserting that faith or belief is not a matter of volition, but a matter of evidence. But I am not asking any one to believe without evidence. I am asking him simply to give its rightful force to the evidence. It is not for want of evidence that any earnest, consecrated seeker is failing to believe that Christ is able and willing to sanctify him wholly, and to do it now. He asserts it in many forms and repeats it again and again as His Divine will that His people should be holy, and if He is not able to make them holy here and now, His omnipotence is impugned, and if He is not willing to make them holy here and now, He must desire them to continue longer in sin, which thought would impugn His own holiness.

No, it is not for want of evidence, but because the faith-faculty has become weakened and paralyzed by sin, and now we must determine to believe, by putting our will on to the side of faith, and allowing it, no longer, to remain on the side of unbelief. Many a seeking soul has come out into the fullness of salvation by singing the hymn:

"I can, I will, I do believe
That Jesus saves me now."

The man who came to Jesus with his right hand withered, was told to stretch it forth. He might have said where is my evidence that it will do any good to try? But he put his will into the obedient attitude. He willed to stretch it forth, and made the effort, and with the obedient will the power came from Jesus, and he stretched it forth and was restored. To every one of weak and paralyzed faith, I say, nay, Jesus says, "Stretch forth thy hand of faith, I am here to be responsible for the result." Believe and receive and confess and rejoice. Beloved, we are sanctified by faith. Glory to the Lamb.

CHAPTER XVI.

CONCLUSION.

I trust it has been sufficiently demonstrated that the doctrine and experience of entire sanctification are fully and clearly taught in Holy Scripture. All the way from the patriarchs to the apostles in the law, in the types, in the Psalms, in the prophets, in the history, in the gospels, in the epistles, we find that God requires His people to be holy and to be holy now, that He makes it, therefore, their privilege to be holy, and that He has made ample provision, in the sacrificial offering of Christ, for them to be made holy.

"For their sakes," says the blessed Saviour, "I sanctify Myself that they also might be sanctified through the truth," or as the margin, "truly sanctified," or as the Revised Version, "that they themselves also may be sanctified in truth." The Lord Jesus Christ most assuredly did not need to be made holy, but all His redeemed children being subjects of inbred sin do need it. As for Him, He was the "holy thing" that was to be born of the Virgin Mary. "He knew no sin," He "did no sin," He was "holy, harmless, undefiled and separate from sinners," and, therefore, when He says "I sanctify Myself," He means nothing more nor less than consecrate Myself, or I set Myself apart, but in the other clause where the term sanctify is used in reference to His people, it must mean that they may be cleansed from all sin entirely sanctified, made holy or pure in heart. He sets Himself apart, therefore, to the work of redemption and salvation that He may have a holy people on earth, as without controversy He must and will have a holy people in heaven.

We have shown that entire sanctification is coetaneous with the baptism with the Holy Ghost, in fact, that the two experiences are in an important sense identical, or, at least, so related to each other that whoever has one has the other. It is Christ and none other who baptizes with the Holy. Ghost. "He shall baptize you with the Holy Ghost and fire," not as some imagine, I think erroneously, that there are to be two baptisms, first that of the Holy Ghost, and afterwards that of fire in the way of affliction or persecution, though plenty of these are promised and experienced by those who would live godly in Christ Jesus, but simply that He shall baptize you with the Holy Ghost under the similitude of fire, that is, that dross and tin and reprobate silver, or, in a word, all inbred sin may be consumed.

Nor is it correct to say that there are "many baptisms" of the Spirit. The Holy Ghost baptism is received by the consecrated believer once for all, and is never repeated unless by unfaithfulness or backsliding he falls from the precious grace which this baptism confers upon him, from Christ through the Spirit, and again comes in repentance and confession to do his first works, and again to be filled with the Spirit and cleansed from all sin. And even in that case the Holy Ghost seldom or never repeats Himself, by giving the same emotional experience as at first, but may and must be received and retained by faith, and the amount of feeling and the kind of feeling which He will arouse must be left to Himself entirely, I mean to say that the experience may be lost and may be regained, but seldom with the same phenomena of consciousness as at the first. Do not speak, then, of having had many baptisms of the Spirit, but seek and find the one baptism with the Holy Ghost and fire. Do not say that you are desiring or that you have had a fresh baptism with the Holy Ghost, but let your thoughts and prayers be directed to the one baptism which cleanseth and endueth and anointeth.

But I would not be misunderstood on this point. The Psalmist says, "I shall be anointed with fresh oil," and to every sanctified child of God, there may and do come seasons of refreshing, also of girding and filling, and fresh anointing for particular services, which are sometimes called fresh baptisms, but which are not to be confounded with the one true abiding Pentecostal experience. These blessings are not to be undervalued or lightly esteemed, but they come because we already have the Blesser Himself as a personal indwelling Presence and Power.

Many teachers of holiness inculcate the doctrine that we are first sanctified by the blood of Jesus, and afterwards filled or baptized with the Holy Ghost. This opinion would necessitate three separate experiences, where, I think, the Scripture only speaks of two. We should have (1) pardon, (2) entire sanctification by the blood, and (3) the filling of the Spirit. There would thus be a separation between the removing of inbred sin from the heart, and the baptism with the Holy Ghost. This baptism would, then, be only a qualification for service. It is regarded by these teachers, as only given for an enduement of power, to do the work to which we are called. And the practical result of this error, for such with due deference I must regard it, is that some will be very anxious to obtain the baptism with the Holy Ghost to make them strong or powerful in their work, but will ignore, or even deny, the doctrine of entire sanctification. Dr. S. A. Keen tells us of a minister who wrote to him that he did not take much stock in sanctification, but that he was very desirous of the Holy Ghost baptism, in order that he might have increased power in the ministry of the word. And, indeed, this seems to be a very prevalent idea, that we are to be baptized for service, but not for cleansing.

I trust that no reader who has followed me through the different chapters of this book will imagine, for a moment, that I under-value, in the slightest degree, the precious blood of Christ, nor do I forget that it is that blood which, as we walk in the light, cleanseth us from all sin. I think I have sufficiently stated elsewhere that the blood of Jesus is the procuring cause of our sanctification, as well as of our justification, and that we are forever dependent upon the atonement for the one blessing as well as the other. The blood of the Son of God is the ground of our sanctification, but it is the Holy Spirit who is the effective agent in destroying the depravity of our hearts.

It is true that our Saviour received the Holy Ghost, and that God anointed Him for the great work of redemption. And in His case, the word used is anointed or descended, and not in any place baptized. He needed not the work of entire sanctification, and, therefore, He is not said to have been baptized with the Holy Ghost. As a man, He did need the energizing for His work, and, therefore, He is said to have been anointed. Beloved, let us not separate what God has joined together. The entire sanctification of the heart and the Holy Ghost baptism are coetaneous experiences, and must not be divorced.

And now, beloved reader, I have accomplished my task. I have shown that like a golden thread the doctrine of entire sanctification runs through the Bible, from Genesis to Revelation. It is found in patriarchal times, it is in the law and the prophets, the types and the ceremonies, the gospels and epistles, everywhere showing us that we have to do with a Holy God, and that we as His children are required to be holy men and women.

To all who shall read this book, I testify that by the grace of God, and the blood of Christ, and the sin-consuming baptism with the Holy Ghost, this poor man, the chief of sinners, is saved to the uttermost. Glory to His name.

And to you, my readers, I bid farewell, and say, May He "make you perfect, stablish, strengthen, settle you." Amen.

www.ingramcontent.com/pod-product-compliance
Lightning Source LLC
Chambersburg PA
CBHW032003040426
42448CB00006B/474